& Unknown

Vampires

by Stuart A. Kallen

ReferencePoint
Press™

San Diego, CA

For more information, contact:
ReferencePoint Press, Inc.
PO Box 27779
San Diego, CA 92198
www.ReferencePointPress.com

Picture credits:
cover: Dreamstime
AP Images: 7, 8, 13, 41, 51, 58, 73
Joe Bernier: 22
Fortean Picture Library: 76, 81
Istockphoto.com: 19, 25, 46
Photos.com: 52
North Wind: 17, 31, 35, 62–63

Series design and book layout:
Amy Stirnkorb

LIBRARY OF CONGRESS CATALOGING-IN-PUBLICATION DATA

Kallen, Stuart A., 1955-
Vampires / by Stuart A. Kallen.
    p. cm. -- (The mysterious & unknown)
    Includes bibliographical references and index.

ISBN-13: 978-1-60152-029-6 (hardback)
ISBN-10: 1-60152-029-8 (hardback)
1. Vampires. I. Title.
BF1556.K35 2008

398'.45--dc22   2007037706

CONTENTS

FOREWORD

"Strange is our situation here upon earth."
—*Albert Einstein*

Since the beginning of recorded history, people have been perplexed, fascinated, and even terrified by events that defy explanation. While science has demystified many of these events, such as volcanic eruptions and lunar eclipses, some remain outside the scope of the provable. Do UFOs exist? Are people abducted by aliens? Can some people see into the future? These questions and many more continue to puzzle, intrigue, and confound despite the enormous advances of modern science and technology.

It is these questions, phenomena, and oddities that Reference-Point Press's *The Mysterious & Unknown* series is committed to exploring. Each volume examines historical and anecdotal evidence as well as the most recent theories surrounding the topic in debate. Fascinating primary source quotes from scientists, experts, and eyewitnesses as well as in-depth sidebars further inform the text. Full-color illustrations and photos add to each book's visual appeal. Finally, source notes, a bibliography, and a thorough index provide further reference and research support. Whether for research or the curious reader, *The Mysterious & Unknown* series is certain to satisfy those fascinated by the unexplained.

INTRODUCTION

The Bloodsuckers

In the early morning hours of March 9, 2007, a man named Miroslav crept through the Serbian night carrying a sledgehammer and a long, sharpened stake made from hawthorn wood. Miroslav, who describes himself as a vampire hunter, was in the yard of deceased Serbian dictator Slobodan Milošević's home in Pozarevac, Serbia. Milošević, who had died a year earlier, was buried in the garden. After kneeling over the grave, Miroslav centered the stake and pounded it down hard, aiming for the dead man's lifeless heart. Satisfied that he had prevented the return of Milošević as a bloodsucking vampire, the slayer sneaked off into what he called the "witching time of night when churchyards yawn."[1]

Milošević, widely known as the Butcher of the Balkans for his part in the killing of tens of thousands of people in Bosnia, Croatia, and Kosovo in the 1990s, was charged by the International

Hunting vampires is
part of a tradition
that dates back
at least a 1,000
years to a time
when cadavers were
commonly said to
rise from the dead
to suck the blood
from human beings.

Criminal Tribunal of the United Nations with war crimes and crimes against humanity. For vampire hunter Miroslav, the anniversary of Milošević's death, which occurred on March 11, 2006, seemed a perfect time to strike. Local tradition holds that the undead climb out of their graves after one year to obtain immortality by drinking the warm blood of the living.

Everybody Loves Dracula

In Serbia and the surrounding nations of eastern Europe, Milošević is hardly the first person to receive a stake through the heart. Hunting vampires is part of a tradition that dates back at least 1,000 years to a time when cadavers were commonly believed to rise from the dead to suck the blood from human beings and other living things. These creatures had pale, bluish skin, skeletal faces, long canine teeth, or fangs, and wore the rotting rags of the decomposed clothing they were buried in. The undead, reanimated corpses who only roamed at night, were called *vampiors* in Serbia, *vámpirs* in Hungary, and vampires in England. The term came into widespread use in the mid-1700s when it was used in government reports concerning attacks on Serbian peasants by the undead. The handsome vampire, with his courtly demeanor is a relatively recent phenomenon, first described by Irish writer Bram Stoker in his famous 1897 novel *Dracula:*

> [He was] a tall old man, clean shaven save for a long white moustache, and clad in black from head to foot, without a single speck of color about him anywhere. . . . His face was a strong, a very strong, aquiline, with high bridge of the thin nose and peculiarly arched nostrils, with lofty domed

forehead, and hair growing scant-ily round the temples but profuse-ly elsewhere. His eyebrows were very massive, almost meeting over the nose, and with bushy hair that seemed to curl in its own profu-sion. The mouth, so far as I could see it under the heavy moustache, was fixed and rather cruel-looking, with peculiarly sharp white teeth. These protruded over the lips, whose re-markable ruddiness showed aston-ishing vitality in a man of his years. For the rest, his ears were pale, and at the tops extremely pointed. The chin was broad and strong, and the cheeks firm though thin.[2]

Milošević, pictured here, was widely known as the Butcher of the Balkans for his part in the killing of tens of thousands of people in Bosnia, Croatia, and Kosovo in the 1990s. Some believed he was a vampire.

This image of an undead bloodsucker was widely popularized in a London play produced by Stoker in 1900 and in dozens of silent films made in Europe and the United States between 1909 and 1928. Dracula later underwent a Hollywood makeover when he was famously portrayed by actor Bela Lugosi in the 1931 film *Dracula*. With his tuxedo, top hat, opera cape, and manners of a suave, Hungarian nobleman, the murderous prince of vampires lost the hairy palms and sharply pointed fingernails described by Stoker. Since that time, millions of people have seen Lugosi-like vampires in horror films, comedies, televisions shows, plays, novels, and even comic books. So pervasive is this creature of the night that so-called vampire cults have developed in many

Bela Lugosi played Dracula in the 1931 film Dracula. *With his tuxedo, top hat, opera cape, and manners of a suave, Hungarian nobleman, the murderous prince of vampires lost the hairy palms and sharply pointed fingernails described by Bram Stoker.*

places throughout the world, including New York, London, and Toronto. Participants paint their faces white and wear silk capes like the fictional Count Dracula or black velvet dresses like Dracula's bride. Some even sharpen their teeth into fangs and claim they need to drink human blood to remain alive.

Cannibalism, Corpses, and Random Attacks

The first written reference to wicked vampires comes from a Russian priest in 1047, but at that time the idea of a corpse that feasted on the human life force was already thousands of years old. Ancient legends from India, Asia, and Africa describe all manner of vile, blood-drinking monsters. These foul-smelling creatures are sent to earth by evil deities to commit unspeakable acts on babies, pregnant women, and other innocent victims.

Vampires may be a product of the imagination or a result of age-old fears buried deep in the human psyche. Or, as some believe, vampires may be as real as the trees in the forest, and those who ignore them do so at their own peril. Whatever the case, vampire culture has become immortal, kept alive by Transylvania travel tours, vampire fashion fans, and people who claim to be the modern version of the ancient blood-drinking creature. For those who live in the world of vampires the realm of the undead is both mysterious and entertaining, and with romantic figures like Dracula leading the way, chances are the bloodsucking buffet will never end.

CHAPTER 1

An Ancient Creature

Throughout the ages, foul and barbaric supernatural creatures called vampires have been said to prey on the innocent, sucking dry their life force. The victims are either left to die or they become vampires themselves. Descriptions of these hideous bloodsuckers have been passed from generation to generation by word of mouth, authors have written books about them, authorities have pursued them, and scholars have attempted to study them. While the details vary, the basic description remains the same. At night, vampirish fiends creep from their graves to spread fear throughout the countryside. Describing this phenomenon in *The Vampire,* eccentric clergyman and supernatural scholar Montague Summers wrote in 1928 that the vampire tradition is worldwide and of dateless antiquity:

Assyria knew the vampire long ago, and he lurked amid the primeval forests of Mexico before [sixteenth-century Spanish explorer Hernán] Cortes came. He is feared by the Chinese, by the Indian, and the Malay alike; whilst Arabian story tells us again and again of the ghouls who haunt ill-omened sepulchers and lonely cross-ways to attack and devour the unhappy traveler.[3]

These creatures are not the elegant, seductive Dracula-like vampires of popular fiction. They are predators in the form of decaying corpses, winged demons, half animals, or even beautiful, malevolent women. They are called revenants, dead bodies that have come back to life.

Magicians and Witches

Basic to all vampire legends is the belief that the dead continue to live, can influence events on earth, and exercise the powers of life and death over human beings. This concept dates back to ancient Africa where deceased ancestors were said to cause pain and sickness among the living if they were not respectfully worshipped with frequent rituals. Those not honored might practice vampiric behavior, causing a mysterious loss of blood in victims, leading to death.

While dead relatives might be pacified with reverential rituals, certain members of the community, such as magicians, were said to retain their evil powers even in death. Since they could not be mollified with respectful worship, the corpses of conjurors

and sorcerers were dealt with in a brutal manner so they could not suck the blood from the living. Their cadavers were chopped apart, the heads were removed, and the limbs severed.

If dead magicians were troublesome, living witches were said to pose an even greater threat. Among the Dahomean people of West Africa, witches, called *obayifo,* were capable of harnessing supernatural powers that allowed them to secretly bleed victims from afar. The wicked *obayifo* were physically indistinguishable from other people, but they could leave their bodies at night and fly great distances as glowing balls of light. In this ghostly form, the witches attacked people, especially children, and sucked their bodies dry of blood.

Stories of blood-drinking witches are common elsewhere in Africa although they differ from region to region. In 1906, Rhodesian army major Arthur Glyn Leonard wrote about the Ibo people in Nigeria, who told him that witches routinely traveled at night to meet with demons; together they plotted ways to kill their neighbors. According to Leonard, death was accomplished by "gradually sucking the blood of the victim through some supernatural and invisible means, the effect of which on the victim is imperceptible to others."[4] The Ibos believed that this form of murder was so supernaturally subtle that even the target of the spell was unaware of what was happening, although he or she would feel great pain. Leonard did not believe in vampire witches; he believed the perpetrators were using poison to slowly kill their victims.

Fears of vampiric spell casters are not confined to Africa. In Serbia and Romania many people believe that dead witches and magicians can rise from the grave to terrorize the living. As in Africa, the corpses of people thought to be evil magicians are decapitated or mutilated after death so they will not rise again.

To diminish the potential powers of the undead, people in some cultures perform specific blood rituals at death. One of the earliest written records of this practice came from Captain James Cook (pictured), who traveled to New Zealand in 1813. Cook saw a woman wailing and cutting herself to draw blood and noticed that most of the natives, called Maoris, had self-inflicted scars. Cook did not realize that the scars were signs of grief and that the Maoris and other Polynesian peoples would ritually cut themselves when mourning the dead.

In Serbia and Romania there is a pervasive belief that dead witches and magicians are prone to rise from the grave to terrorize the living.

Blood Equals Life

Some cultures believe that every cadaver is a potential vampire. To diminish the potential powers of the undead, people in these cultures perform specific blood rituals at death. This is based on the idea that spirits of the dead need the life force contained in blood to remain vital and alive in the next world. One of the earliest written records of this practice came from Captain James Cook who traveled to New Zealand in 1813. Cook saw a woman wailing and cutting herself to draw blood and noticed that most of the natives, called Maoris, had self-inflicted scars on arms, cheeks, or thighs. Cook did not realize that the scars were signs of grief and that the Maoris and other Polynesian peoples used to ritually cut themselves when mourning the dead. In later years, Westerners came to understand the significance of such rituals, explained by Summers:

> If they are not willing to feed [the corpse] with their blood he will come back and take it from them, so naturally it is believed to be far better to give without [protest] and gain the protection of the ghost, rather than refuse what the phantom will inevitably seize upon in vengeance and in wrath. . . . These practices then . . . have more than a touch of vampirism, the essence of which consists of the belief that the dead man is able to sustain semi-life by . . . drinking the blood of the living."[5]

The vampiric idea that blood equals life has played out differently in other cultures. Among the ancient Aztecs, inhabitants of what is now Mexico, it was thought that drinking the blood—or eating the hearts—of enemies provided warriors with immortality.

In some parts of the world, however, blood is feared rather than revered. In New Guinea, there is a long-standing conviction that even a few drops of spilled blood will attract evil spirits who can gain power over humans by drinking it. While there are some today who ignore this ancient belief, traditionalists in New Guinea continue to cover their blood with dirt after an accident and burn clothing and bandages that have been stained with blood.

Demons and Deities

The belief in evil spirits is found in all cultures, and many demons from ancient mythology share traits with vampires. More than 5,000 years ago, the Mesopotamians, who lived in what is now Iraq feared a creature called the Akhkharu, a female demon said to roam the night, drinking the blood of newborn babies and pregnant women. This ancient vampire was part of a complex Mesopotamian mythology that included seven such evil spirits, descriptions of whom have been found on stone tablets. One poem from antiquity, translated by anthropologist R. Campbell Thompson in 1903, describes the vampires:

> Seven are they! Seven are they!
> Spirits that minish [make small] the heaven and earth
> That minish the land . . .
> Of giant strength and giant tread
> Demons (like raging bulls, great ghosts) . . .
> Knowing no mercy they rage against mankind
> They spill their blood like rain
> Devouring . . . flesh (and) sucking . . . veins
> They are demons full of violence, ceaselessly devouring blood.[6]

Several thousand years later, the Mesopotamian demons reappeared in ancient Greek culture, and the myths of the ancient Greeks include dozens of blood-drinking deities. One of the most feared Greek vampires was a witch bearing the name of the screech owl, or *strix*. Like the owl, the strix flies through the night but instead of eating rodents and snakes, she attacks and kills babies by sucking their blood. In this manner, the screeching vampire witch has a close resemblance to the Mesopotamian Akhkharu.

Another type of Greek vampire, the lamiai, are named after a mortal woman Lamia, who sought revenge on the human race. Lamia was the queen of Libya and mistress of the Greek god Zeus. However, Zeus's wife, Hera, became jealous of the relationship and killed all of Lamia's children who were fathered by Zeus. Because the mortal Lamia could not fight back against Hera, she struck back by killing the children of human mothers, usually by drinking their blood.

The blood sucking transformed Lamia into a revolting monster who spawned a number of demonic beings in her image. These lamiai were ugly and deformed. Their lower bodies had a snake-like appearance but the creatures had two feet, one made from brass, the other shaped like the foot of a goat, ox, or donkey. Like Lamia, the monsters thrived on the blood of babies, and they could also shift their shape into that of a beautiful woman who would first attract—then kill—young men.

Gory Ghouls of India

The ancient Hindu texts of India also contain a host of vampiric deities and supernatural entities similar to those found in Mesopotamia. For example, ogres called *rakshasas* prey upon the blood of infants and pregnant women. The creatures live in cemeteries,

Another type of vampire, the lamiai, are named after a mortal woman named Lamia, who sought revenge on the human race. Lamia was the queen of Libya and mistress of the Greek god Zeus (pictured). However, Zeus's wife, Hera, became jealous of the relationship and killed all of Lamia's children who were fathered by Zeus. Because the mortal Lamia could not fight back against Hera, she struck back by killing the children of human mothers, usually by drinking their blood.

where they disrupt the rituals of people honoring their ancestors. They are also shape-shifters, meaning they can assume various forms, including animal or half animal, half human.

The rakshasas support many other unsavory characters. Sorcerers called *yatu-dhana* feed on the bloody remains of the victims killed by the rakshasas. Even more horrible are repugnant ghouls called *pisachas*, a word that translates as "eaters of raw flesh." These blood-thirsty creatures feast on the putrefied remains left behind by the yatu-dhana and in doing so spread plagues and deadly diseases.

The supreme deity, Brahma, is said to have created pisachas in anger—after rakshasas began to drink his blood and eat his body. As ancient Hindu texts explain, after creating gods, demons, and humans, Brahma saw the rakshasas, and "he was displeased, and his hair fell out and became serpents. And when he saw the serpents he was angry, and the creatures born of his anger were the fierce flesh-eating *pisachas.* Thus Brahma created cruel and gentle creatures."[7]

Other cruel creatures of Indian lore include *bhuta,* the souls of the insane, the murdered, and the diseased. These unfortunate beings exist as sinister shadows or foggy ghosts that live around crematoriums, cemeteries, deserted regions, and abandoned buildings. As they wander the night, the bhuta can enter cadavers and bring them to life in a zombielike form of existence. The re-animated corpses have long, lolling black tongues, and they stalk the night, slitting open the bodies of victims with their razor-sharp talons, devouring the intestines, and drinking the spilled blood. Bhuta are also shape-shifters and can transform into bats or owls. Perhaps this is why Indians believe it is unlucky to hear an owl hoot, especially when standing in a cemetery.

A different type of bhuta, called a *churel,* is created from

One creature of Indian lore includes bhuta, the souls of the insane, the murdered, and the diseased. As they wander the night, the bhuta enter cadavers and bring them to life in a zombielike form of existence. The reanimated corpses have long, lolling black tongues, and they stalk the night, slitting open the bodies of victims with their razor-sharp talons, devouring the intestines and drinking the spilled blood. Bhuta are also shape-shifters and can transform themselves into bats or owls.

Did You
Know?

In India vampires called *bhuta* stalk the night, slitting open the bodies of victims with their razor-sharp talons.

women who die unnatural deaths through murder, suicide, or accident. If these victims are not treated respectfully by their relatives, their spirits return to drink the blood of the men in the family. To carry out this deed, the churel assumes the disguise of a beautiful maiden. The masquerade does not always work, however, as it is said that the feet of churels are backwards, with the heels in the front and the toes in back. Whatever the case, after striking a victim, churels revert to repulsive demon form with pig's faces, huge fangs, clawlike hands, and a potbelly.

Churels sometimes work in tandem with the major Hindu goddess Kali, a deity with black skin, fangs, and four arms who wears a garland of corpses and skulls. Kali, known as the destroyer, haunts battlegrounds where she gets drunk on the blood of the dead and dying. Kali loves blood so much, according to nineteenth-century British explorer and author, Sir Richard Burton, when she is unable to find victims "to satisfy her thirst for the curious juice, [she] cut her own throat that the blood might spout up into her mouth."[8]

The Gypsy Influence

In the Middle Ages, the vampires of Eastern mythology were introduced to the West by the Romany people, commonly known as Gypsies, who migrated from northern India to Europe about 1,000 years ago. These nomadic people lived in Greece, Germany, Romania, and the Slavic-speaking nations of Hungary, Russia, Poland, Slovenia, and Serbia. The Gypsies were undoubtedly acquainted with Indian vampiric deities, which they reworked into their own religious beliefs.

The Romany in the Balkans believed that when someone died his or her soul hovered near the corpse in the burial ground. However, like the Indian bhuta, the soul might become restless and reenter the corpse, causing it to rise from the grave. To prevent this from happening, families performed highly structured funeral rites and remained diligent about visiting graves of ancestors year after year. Despite this attention to the dead, it was thought to be inevitable that some cadavers would live on as vampires, called *mulo,* meaning "one who is dead." As with Indian vampirism, suicides and murder victims were particularly prone to becoming mulos, as were those who did not receive proper funeral rites.

Some Romany vampires looked normal except for one odd physical trait, such as a missing finger, or animal-like limb. Believers among the Gypsies of Germany and Slovenia say that vampires look normal but have a jellylike appearance, since they have left their bones behind in the grave. Other vampires, however, looked like dead bodies that had partially decomposed. Whatever their form, the creatures would either emerge after midnight or at noon, when no one could see that they cast no shadow.

These vampires might make their presence known by destroying property and making horrid noises, including shrieking, shrill scratching, pounding, and thumping. Male vampires were said to sexually assault wives, girlfriends, or other women. Female vampires were said to appear normal and might even marry. However, the husband would be driven mad by the demands of his insatiable wife.

The Romany belief in vampires was not limited to humans; it was also said that horses, snakes, dogs, cats, sheep, and even chickens could return from the dead to harass the living. These animals became vampiric through interaction with the dead. For example, a cat that walked over a cadaver or jumped into an unfilled grave would become a deadly, bloodsucking feline. Inanimate objects

Romania and Transylvania

Ukraine

Hungary

Moldova

Vlad
Birthplace

Dumbraveni Sighisoara

Bacau

Bran
Castle

Ukraine

Transylvania

Buzau

Brasov

Danube River

Tirgoviste

Romania

Bucharest

Black
Sea

Yugoslavia

Bulgaria

Source: www.transylvania-tours.com, 2007.

*This map shows the Transylvania region of Romania, birthplace of
Vlad "the Impaler" Dracula and the place author Bram Stoker chose
as the setting for his fictional vampire tale Dracula.*

were also prone to vampirism. A rotting pumpkin or squash might begin to ooze blood if not discarded. Even a rope used to yoke animals could become a vampire if left untied and unused for more than three years.

The Living and the Dead

The Romany were traveling entertainers who journeyed across Europe. Wherever they went, they took their stories with them and some of these stories were adopted by other cultures. This was particularly true in eastern Europe, in a region called Transylvania. This region, in north-central Romania, was once part of the Austro-Hungarian Empire. In his book *Vampires,* journalist and former gravedigger Bob Curran describes Transylvania as being filled with "images of ruined castles, and . . . lofty, mist-swathed East European crags; of deep dark forests, filled with wolves and all manner of unspeakable horrors."[9]

Transylvania is home to Bram Stroker's famous vampire character Dracula, but the author derived much of his story from an 1888 book *The Land Beyond the Forest* by Emily Gerard, a Scottish woman who lived in Transylvania in the 1880s. Gerard describes several supernatural entities that were said to live in the area, including *nosferatu,* a word that means "undead" in Romanian:

> [Decidedly] evil is the *nosferatu,* or vampire, in which every Roumanian peasant believes as firmly as he does in heaven or hell. There are two sorts of vampires, living and dead. The living vampire is generally the illegitimate offspring of two illegitimate persons; but even a flawless pedigree

will not insure any one against the intrusion of a vampire into the family vault, since every person killed by a nosferatu becomes likewise a vampire after death.[10]

The concept of vampires both living and dead is derived from legends brought to Romania by the Romans in the second century A.D. Roman beliefs were based on ancient Greek mythology and the Greek strix became the Roman *striga vie,* or live blood-sucking witch, while the *strigoi mort* were dead vampires. The live witches, recognized by their red faces and full red lips, created havoc by sending their souls out to kill locals. They also frolicked in the moonlight performing macabre dances with the *strigoi mort.*

Over the centuries, the two types of vampires merged into a single creature, the *strigoi,* also known by the old Greek term for nosferatu, *nosophoros,* or plague carrier. When Gypsy beliefs were added to the mix, the modern image of vampires emerged, the bloodsucking revenant that drained the blood of its victim either causing death or converting the prey from a living human into an undead nosferatu.

Infesting Hamlets and Villages

The most famous vampire in Romania, Dracula, is a fictional character invented by Bram Stoker. However, the author based his Count Dracula on a real person, Vlad Dracula III, "the Impaler." Dracula ruled Wallachia, a principality bordering Transylvania, on three separate occasions between 1448 and 1476. Dracula's reigns were brutal and bloody—his favorite method of disposing of enemies was to have them impaled on long wooden stakes where they slowly bled to death.

Bran Castle, where Vlad the Impaler spent his days torturing and killing thousands of people, is located in the Transylvania area of Romania and is a major tourist destination as many believe the legend of Dracula began with Vlad and his castle.

Nosferatu, a word
that means "undead"
in Romanian, is
another term for
vampire.

Dracula was accused of cannibalism and blood drinking in widely circulated books and pamphlets even before his death in 1476. By the 1500s, Dracula was widely spoken of as a vampire in league with the devil, and his reign was associated with vampirism, especially by those who suffered his wrath.

In the years that followed, the ancient superstitions about vampires remained very much alive, exploding into a continent-wide panic in the eighteenth century. The hysteria began in Kisilova, Serbia, in 1725, when a peasant named Peter Plogojowitz was said to have come back as a vampire after his death, sucking the blood from nine villagers. Local officials investigated the reports and concluded that the deaths were unrelated to vampires. However, details of the accusations were published in official reports, and these were excerpted in several popular newspapers. The news reports failed to mention that vampires were not involved the deaths. The spurious information fueled reports of vampires throughout Germany, Italy, France, England, and Spain. At the height of the frenzy, thousands of eyewitnesses claimed to have seen bloodsucking vampires roaming streets, alleyways, and the rural countryside. In Serbia, Prussia, Poland, and Romania, terrified villagers invaded graveyards; dug up, or exhumed, decaying cadavers; and drove stakes into their hearts.

The mutilation of the dead, most of whom were buried as Christians, alarmed church officials in Rome, who launched an investigation into vampirism. The results of this inquiry appeared in a 1744 book, *Dissertation on the Vampiri* by Giuseppe Davanzati, the archbishop of Trani, Italy. After a five-year study of official reports about vampire sightings and activities, mostly in Germany between 1720 and 1739, the archbishop concluded that vampires were not real. Instead, they were an illusion or a

Vampires
of India

The folklore of India is rife with vampiric entities. In *Vampires* Bob Curran describes the picky eating habits of several disgusting entities called rakshasas:

> [A] type of rakshasa, the *bramaparush*
> . . . had an appetite for human intes-
> tines, wrapping them around its body
> and performing a ritualistic dance. An-
> other vampiric entity, the *jigarkhwar,*
> found in the Sind area of India, was at-
> tracted, not by intestines, but by blood
> and liver, which it consumed after para-
> lyzing its victim with a mesmeric stare
> that couldn't be avoided no matter how
> hard the prey tried to look away.

Bob Curran, *Vampires*. Franklin Lakes, NJ: New Page, 2005, p. 141.

fantasy, possibly generated by mass hysteria. While Davanzati believed the panic itself might have had diabolical origins, the pope advised church leaders to calm the public and speak out against the desecration of the dead.

Even as Davanzati was preparing his report, a renowned French Bible scholar of the Benedictine order, Dom Augustin Calmet, was doing his own research into vampirism. The resulting book, published in 1746 with the typically long titles of the time, was called *Essays on the Appearances of the Angels, the Demons and the Spirits, and on the Ghosts and Vampires of Hungary, of Bohemia, of Moravia and Silesia.* In the book, Calmet describes the situation in eastern Europe:

> [We] are told that dead men, men who have been dead for several months, I say, returned from the tomb, are heard to speak, walk about, infest hamlets and villages, injure both men and animals, whose blood they drain thereby making them sick and ill, and at length actually causing death. Nor can men deliver themselves from these terrible visitations, nor secure themselves from these horrid attacks, unless they dig the corpses up from the graves [and] drive a sharp stake through their bodies. . . . The name given to these ghosts is Oupires, or Vampires, that is to say, bloodsuckers.[11]

Despite the official reports he discovered during his research, Calmet spends considerable time challenging the existence of vampires, using religious doctrine to analyze the exact physical nature of the bloodsuckers. He questions how a dead body could leave a coffin, travel through six feet of dirt, kill a victim, and return to the grave without ever disturbing the soil. To do so, vampires must be spirits, like ghosts, that can pass through solid objects, later assuming a fantastical body that is only seen by victims. If true, based on Christian doctrine, Calmet states that vampirism could only be the work of the devil. "The devil can endue [endow] these corpses with sub-

tlety and bestowed upon them the power of passing through the earth . . . of becoming rarefied as air or water to penetrate the earth."[12] However, this concept presented a theological problem for Calmet since such powers are not attributed to Satan in the Bible.

Besides lacking biblical proof, Calmet discounts most vampire stories since they were generated by illiterate peasants, "folk who were very ignorant, very credulous, very superstitious, and brimful of all kinds of wonderful stories concerning [vampires]."[13] However, Calmet refuses to say vampires do not exist since he cannot find any alternative reasons to explain the supernatural phenomena that had been occurring in eastern Europe for centuries:

> [The] particulars which are related [to vampires] are so singular, so detailed, accompanied with circumstances so probable and so likely, as well as with the most weighty and well-attested legal

To calm the vampire hysteria in the 1750s, Austrian empress Maria Theresa issued edicts that forbade the opening of graves and the desecration of bodies.

deposition that it seems impossible not to subscribe to the belief which prevails in these countries that these Apparitions do actually come forth from their graves and that they are able to produce the terrible effects which are so widely and so positively attributed to them.[14]

Although it was contradictory in nature, *Vampires of Hungary, of Bohemia, of Moravia and Silesia* quickly became a best seller throughout Europe. While generating intense criticism from religious scholars and intellectuals, the popularity of the book was based on the frightening stories extracted from official reports, eyewitness accounts, newspaper stories, travelogues, and evidence presented by church officials. With no intention of doing so, Calmet fueled the fires of the vampire panic, creating a new outbreak of hysteria in the Austro-Hungarian Empire. This outraged Austrian empress Maria Theresa, who ordered her personal physician to look into the matter. He quickly wrote a report calling vampirism "supernatural quackery"[15] while denouncing the mutilation of bodies.

Based on these findings, the empress took the matter of vampirism away from the church, issuing edicts in 1757 that forbade the opening of graves and the desecration of bodies. This put an end to vampire hysteria in eastern Europe.

Condemned to Wander

The belief in vampires remained strong for many centuries. Even in the twenty-first-century world, there are those who fear the evil vampires of ancient legend, according to Curran, creatures "who have lived evil lives or who have committed dark sins, such

In the 1740s, due to vampire mania, Austrian empress Maria Theresa took the matter of vampirism away from the church, issuing edicts in 1757 that forbade the opening of graves and the desecration of bodies. This put an end to vampire hysteria in eastern Europe.

as witchcraft, [who] were not admitted to [heaven], but were condemned to wander the world forever . . . witches and warlocks of rural Romania who often subsist on blood."[16]

CHAPTER 2

The Living, the Dead, and the Undead

Discussing the nature of vampires in England in the 1870s, professor John Scoffern wrote, "The best definition I can give of a vampire is a living, mischievous and murderous dead body. A living dead body! The words are idle, contradictory, incomprehensible, but so are vampires."[17] Scoffern was a scholar of forensic pathology, a branch of medicine concerned with establishing the cause of a death in criminal cases. The fact that vampires were perplexing to someone with his expertise illustrates their mysterious nature. And for centuries experts like Scoffern have asked, how does a seemingly normal person transform into a blood-drinking corpse, and why does this happen to some unlucky souls and not to others? Like many other aspects of vampirism, the answers are as varied as the individual vampires themselves.

Born Under a Bad Sign

In some parts of Europe people once believed that certain individuals were destined to become vampires by the conditions of their birth. During the Middle Ages, when people had no knowledge of science or medicine, some birth defects were perceived as evil omens that could lead to becoming a vampire. In Romania, children were expected to return as vampires upon death if they were born with teeth, an extra nipple, excessive hair, deformed limbs, a split lower lip, a large birthmark (especially on the face), or a small tail at the base of the spine. In 1639, writers George Chapman and James Shirley describe a newborn unlucky enough to have several vampiric signs:

> He was born with teeth in his head . . . and hath one
> toe on his left foot crooked, and in the form of an
> eagle's talon. . . . What shall I say? Branded, marked,
> and designed in his birth for shame and obloquy
> [disgrace], which appeareth further, by a mole un-
> der his right ear, with only three witch's hairs in it;
> strange and ominous predictions of nature![18]

This unfortunate baby was promptly taken to a fire specially lit on the town square where the soles of his feet were held in the flames. This was meant to prevent him from turning into a vampire at some later date.

A child born with a red caul, a harmless, thin membrane that covers the face of the newborn, also created fear. Although a caul was considered good luck in many cultures, thought to give lifelong protection from drowning, in eastern Europe caul bearers were seen as future vampires.

"The best definition I can give of a vampire is a living, mischievous and murderous dead body."

—Forensic scientist John Scoffern discussing the nature of vampires in the 1870s.

While it might be understandable that people with no knowledge of modern science feared newborns with unusual births or physical imperfections, some signs of vampirism were based on pure superstition. Vampires might be traced to the seventh son born to the seventh son in a family. This stems from the magical significance given to the number seven in many cultures along with special powers people are said to inherit through birth order. In some eastern European countries simply being born with red hair was a sign of bloodsucking tendencies, based on the belief that Judas Iscariot, who betrayed Jesus, was a redhead. Commenting on this superstition in 1623, English author John Wodroephe wrote, "It is believed in Serbia, Bulgaria, and Romania, that there are certain red-[haired] vampires who are called 'Children of Judas,' and that these, the foulest of the foul, kill their victim with one bite or kiss which drains the blood as if it were a single draught. The poisoned flesh of the victim is wounded with the Devil's stigmata, three hideous scars shaped thus, XXX."[19]

In such cases, women were blamed for causing vampirism in their babies. The mother of the Judas child might have had a black cat cross her path while pregnant, or unwittingly let a witch gaze upon her. Worst of all, the woman might have conceived outside the bonds of marriage and produced a child that would surely become a vampire.

The Unrepentant and Evil

A person born with so-called marks of the vampire often became an outcast, shunned by society. In such cases, the person might turn to crime, or dabble in the dark arts such as magic and witchcraft to seek revenge on his or her pitiless neighbors. In

In some eastern European countries simply being born with red hair was a sign of bloodsucking tendencies, based on the belief that Judas Iscariot, pictured on the left, who betrayed Jesus, was a redhead.

such cases, the evildoer effectively ensured that he or she would become a bloodsucker after death since it was widely believed that thieves, murderers, prostitutes, witches, and wizards were vampires in training.

Others bearing the purported mark of a vampire might become so despondent that they committed suicide to end their

pain. However, this would provide no relief since it is said that a person who commits suicide will never find rest. As Summers writes, "So great is the horror which the act of suicide . . . inspires in every man of sane mind that it is not at all surprising it should be deemed that the unfortunate wretches who have destroyed themselves become vampires after death."[20]

A person need not be a wizard or commit suicide to become a vampire. Those who led a generally sinful life were said to be doomed to a harsh existence in the afterlife. Such was the case of 60-year-old Johannes Cuntius, an alderman in Pentsch, Silesia, in the sixteenth century. Cuntius was accidentally kicked in the head by a horse one day on his way home from work. He was not killed immediately, but according to parapsychologist Rosemary Ellen Guiley, as he lay dying, he confessed that "his sins were too grievous to be pardoned by God, and that he had made a pact with the Devil."[21] Upon his death several days later, a black cat attacked his face and violently scratched it. The sky immediately filled with clouds and a violent tempest created chaos until Cuntius was buried.

Cuntius had been dead no more than a few days when the spirit of the sinner was said to have risen from the grave and walked into town, molesting village women along the way. During the following weeks, Pentsch authorities were flooded with stories of vampiric activity. It was said that objects flew through the air, people were bitten in their sleep, and loud trampling noises were heard throughout the village. There were many other disturbances as well, as Guiley writes: "The Cuntius specter . . . strangled old men, galloped around the house like a horse, wrestled with people, vomited fire, spotted the church's altar cloth with blood, bashed the heads of dogs against the ground, turned milk into blood, drank up supplies of milk, threw goats about, devoured chickens, and pulled up fence posts. Terrible smells and the sensation of foul, icy breath permeated the Cuntius house."[22]

Hoping to find an answer to the problem, the townspeople inspected the graveyard and found mouse-sized holes around the grave of Cuntius. The holes were filled but appeared again within hours. Finally villagers dug up the body only to discover that Cuntius was a vampire—his cadaver remained soft and pliable and moved about as if it were alive. The corpse was described in the seventeenth century by religion scholar Henry More:

> His Skin was tender and florid, his Joynts not at all stiff, but limber and moveable, and a staff being put into his hand, he grasped it with His fingers very fast; his eyes also of themselves would be one time open, and another time shut; [the villagers] opened a vein in his Leg, and the blood sprang out as fresh as in the living; his Nose was entire and full, not sharp, as in those that are ghastly sick, or quite dead: and yet Cuntius, his body, had [lain] in the grave from Feb. 8 to July 20, which is almost half a year.[23]

The corpse of Cuntius was hauled into court and a formal hearing was held. A judgment of vampirism was rendered against the cadaver and the judge order the body to be burned. Wood was piled high upon Cuntius and set aflame, but the resulting conflagration did not consume the body. A hook was used to pull it from the inferno and an executioner was called to draw and quarter the corpse. However, when the executioner sunk his broadax into

"His Skin was tender and florid, his Joynts not at all stiff, but limber and moveable."

—Religion scholar Henry More describing the corpse of a suspected vampire.

the dead man's body, according to More, "the blood was so pure and spirituous, that it spurted into his face as he cut him."[24] After much effort, Cuntius was finally chopped to pieces, burned, and the ashes thrown in the river. When this was accomplished, More wrote, "the *Spectre* never more appeared."[25]

Nurtured with Great Care

Vampires such as Cuntius are revenants, or dead bodies that have come back to life. These vampires need to suck blood from humans or animals to keep their bodies from decomposing. They do so by biting into the jugular vein in the neck, a process known as the kiss of the vampire. The bloodsucking revenants transform their victims into other revenants who thereafter must commit the same reprehensible deed to survive. This can lead to a vampire epidemic, in which every individual in a town is converted, bite by bite, to vampirism. Those who escape this horrible plague must exhume the undead and drive a stake through the heart of each body.

Rampages by revenants like Cuntius can affect dozens of people, but the blatant nature of the attacks means that the vampire can be easily detected and destroyed. However, there is another breed of bloodsucker that kills in secret and may avoid discovery for decades, or even centuries. These vampires are described as suave and sophisticated and are said to live among the wealthiest and most privileged members of society. Unlike typical revenants, this type of vampire may live in a castle or mansion, sleep in a coffin, have a heightened sense of sight and smell, and be fatally allergic to sunlight. The creature may be centuries old but has lost its soul to achieve the dream of immortality.

Debonair Draculas do not simply bite their prey, drink their blood, and leave them to die. Instead they carefully nurture their victims and teach them the ways of the vampire. The vampires-in-training do not resist their masters since the process allegedly converts them into mindless psychic slaves attached to their victimizers in a sort of blood brotherhood. Believers say the process begins when a vampire attacks a victim and, rather than killing him, drains his blood until he is almost dead. The next day, the bloodsucker reappears and explains to the victim that he has been chosen to become a vampire. At this point, the victim is weakened by the attack and easily mesmerized by the bloodsucker's charisma. In this condition he often chooses to leave his mundane problems behind in order to live an eternal life as an aristocratic vampire. With the consent of the victim, the vampire completes the process, paralyzing him with a vampire's kiss and drinking his blood in a violent ritual. After the rite is finished, the vampire bites its own wrist and allows the disciple to drink blood for the first time. This is said to be a profound awakening for the new vampire who can now perceive colors and shapes with a startling clarity unknown to mortals. However, after the initial joy wears off, the new vampire begins to experience remorse and despair as he presides over the death of his human body and his rebirth as a vampire.

Drawing on her extensive knowledge of vampire folklore and legend, Anne Rice, bestselling author of *Interview with the Vampire,* describes the rest of the initiation process:

> The victim is . . . nurtured with great care, is helped
> to develop the vampire senses until all perception
> vibrates with high sensitivity, is taught to kill, to
> search for a coffin, to travel with one across the

Did You Know?

In vampires, the neurotransmitter dopamine is released in the brain when the creature is feeding on blood, which creates a narcotic, addictive effect.

world without raising suspicion, is taught how to live a wealthy life in the manner of a grand lord or lady. The process of transforming a victim into a vampire can only be described in human terms as a kind of "falling in love."[26]

Becoming a Vampire

Over the centuries, scientists, doctors, and others have tried to explain the physical transformation that is said to occur when a human becomes a vampire, a process sometimes referred to by the unusual word *vampirification*. Normally, when a person dies, the heart and brain stop functioning, chemical changes cause the skin to turn white, and the joints to become stiff with rigor mortis, making body parts difficult to move. Within days the body undergoes decomposition, turning green and shedding nails and hair, with facial features soon becoming unrecognizable. Vampires, according to historical accounts, remain intact, their limbs move, and their bodies experience little decay. They continue to grow hair and nails, their skin is ruddy, and they do not smell of rot. In 1616, Italian scientist Ludovico Fatinelli published *Treatise on Vampires*, in which he attempted to explain these bizarre changes.

According to Fatinelli, when a person is bitten by a vampire, decomposition is forestalled. Instead, the body enters what is called a vampiric coma. During this phase, the pulse slows, breathing is shallow, and the pupils are dilated to such a point that the victim is assumed dead and is often buried. If the person is old, very young, or ill, he or she will probably die a normal death. A young, healthy person, however, will briefly die but awaken after about 24 hours as a full vampire. Within another 24 hours, the vampires begin to hunt.

Anne Rice, best-selling author of Interview with the Vampire, *compares the conversion from mortal to vampire to falling in love.*

When a person
turns into a vampire,
their upper and
lower canine teeth
grow excessively
large, creating
fangs.

Fatinelli never explains how a person in a vampiric coma can climb out of a coffin buried deep beneath the ground. In any event, upon the publication of his book, he was charged with heresy by the church and was burned at the stake for popularizing the notion of vampires.

Red Eyes, Black Blood, and No Heart

It might seem unusual to apply scientific concepts to a mythical creature like a vampire. However, as forensic psychologist Katherine Ramsland explains: "[There] have been numerous attempts to explain different aspects of a vampire's existence within the physical universe. Sometimes it is because someone wants badly to [prove] real vampires do exist, and sometimes it is because [a researcher] wants to . . . prove a powerful myth can be explained within a rational world."[27] As a result, several authors have written books that combine forensic science with biology and folklore to describe the strange process of vampirification. These publications include *Five Books on the Structure of the Vampire Body* written in the sixteenth century by Belgian physician Andreas Vesalius, and more recently, *Clinical Vampirism: Blending Myth and Reality* by Philip D. Jaffe.

According to these sources the transformation begins in the brain. The human brain produces a chemical, or neurotransmitter, called dopamine, which produces feelings of well-being. Addictive drugs such as cocaine trigger the brain to release excessive amounts of dopamine, producing a high. In vampires, researchers say, dopamine is released when the creature feeds on blood. The feeding creates a narcotic, addictive effect and feelings of well-being.

Other changes are said to occur in a vampire's sense organs. For example, the pupils in vampire eyes are superdilated. This makes their eyes appear black but also gives them exceptional night vision. However, dilated pupils would make it nearly impossible for a vampire to see during the day, which is why they are said to hide from sunlight. Another transformation in the eye, an inflammation that makes the whites of their eyes appear red or bloodshot, is said to give vampires their creepy appearance.

The excellent sense of smell attributed to vampires is thought to result from extra receptor cells in the nose and throat. The cells also grow in the ears and give the vampire supersensitive hearing. These changes in the senses make vampires exceptionally hard to capture since they can allegedly see, hear, and smell a hostile person long before that person sees them.

Other changes frequently associated with vampires show up in the hair, skin, teeth, and fingernails. The most obvious change is the growth of the upper and lower canine teeth, which take on the appearance of fangs. Some vampires ostensibly have numerous other sharp teeth, like sharks, and there are legends that certain vampires can retract their teeth so they look normal when not in use. Another persistent legend has it that vampires actually file their teeth to make them razor sharp. In addition, they cultivate long, fast-growing fingernails, filed to razor sharpness so they can grab and hold on to their victims. Other physiological changes described by vampire researchers are less functional and may be a result of the blood diet or simply because vampires live so long. Researchers say new vampires have an unhealthy yellow skin color, but as the skin ages, it becomes translucent and bluish from the veins under the skin becoming visible. Within the veins of a vampire the blood runs cold as would be expected from a formerly dead entity. The vampire's body temperature is also described as much lower than normal human body

Some vampires live
in castles, sleep
in coffins, have
heightened senses
of sight and smell,
and are fatally
allergic to sunlight.

temperature. The temperature of a 100- to 250-year-old vampire may be as low as 65°F (18°C), compared with 98.6°F (37°C) in humans. Temperature decreases with age and in older vampires, between 1,000 to 5,000 years old, body temperature might even sink to 60°F (15.5°C).

Another unusual aspect of vampire blood concerns the color. It is said that because vampires lack a protein in the red blood cells called hemoglobin, their blood is black. One of the earliest records of black blood was recorded in 1196 by a British writer known as William of Newburgh who described an incident at the Melrose Abbey in Scotland. This concerned a dead priest who allegedly turned into a vampire, rose from his tomb at night, and traveled several miles to harass a woman he had known while alive. The woman reported the revenant to church officials, noting that he groaned horribly when he appeared and turned her cow's milk to blood. In order to confirm the story, two sentinels were assigned to watch over the priest's grave.

A few nights later, as one of the sentinels slept on the job, the revenant rose once again. The guard who was awake fought off the vampire with a broadax, leaving a large wound in the body cavity before chasing the creature back to his grave. As the sentinel watched, the grave opened up and swallowed the undead priest. Church officials were called and the churchyard caretakers, called sextons, were ordered to dig up the coffin. When it was unearthed, witnesses reported that the body had a fresh gaping wound, caused by the sentinel's ax, and the casket was overflowing with thick, black blood. The corpse was removed and burned, and the undead cleric was never seen again.

Those who study vampires say that the black blood is pumped not by a heart but by contractions in the skeletal muscles in the chest. This is traced to the belief that vampires either possess no heart or that their hearts are so withered that they only pump once a day. Whatever the case, the skeletal bones and muscles in the chest, like others in the vampire body, are said to become stronger and thicker over time, allowing vampires to move rapidly and gain enormous strength. Another aspect of this extraordinary power and speed is a profusion of adrenaline in vampire blood. This hormone, released in humans during stressful or dangerous situations, is purportedly found in high amounts in vampires. This creates a fearsome aggressiveness allowing the vampire to move so rapidly that its actions may be imperceptible to the human eye.

Age and Experience

By most accounts, vampires have formidable speed, strength, and superhuman powers, which make them skilled hunters of human prey. Their physical attributes may also explain stories of vampires living for hundreds or even thousands of years. Commenting on this aspect of vampirism, Ramsland writes, "It seems that the very condition of being a vampire . . . positively affects the body's . . . endurance and vitality."[28] Ramsland attributes this to what she calls immortalized cells, or microscopic cells within the body that resist aging when fed on a diet of blood. When deprived of blood, however, vampires are said to become ill with flu-like symptoms. If starvation continues, vampires will die. Therefore, it is imperative that vampires learn many skills that permit them to live in a secretive manner while acquiring a steady supply of human blood. In order to do so, they must sharpen their skills, and attain new ones, with each passing year.

Hugo Pecos is someone who has studied aging and the growth

When deprived of blood vampires are said to become ill with flulike symptoms. If starvation continues, vampires will die. In this computer-generated image, a pale vampire, about to bite a woman, appears malnourished.

of experience in vampires. Pecos oversees an organization he calls the Federal Vampire & Zombie Agency (FVZA), which claims responsibility for controlling America's vampire and zombie populations while overseeing scientific research into the undead.

According to Pecos, the first days are the hardest for newborn vampires:

> A newly transformed vampire awakens disoriented, its judgment clouded by competing impulses and memories of its previous life. But all those are drowned out by a fierce, intense desire for blood. This urge for blood eventually snaps a vampire into focus, and it sets about finding a way to fill that urge.[29]

Once this loathsome addiction has been satisfied, the fresh blood acts as a tonic, helping the vampire to focus his mind and move on with his undead life. However, the youngest bloodsuckers, those under 200 years old, are weaklings among vampires. Although they are said to possess three times the strength of humans, they are still apprentices, called fledglings, who remain bound to their masters or sires. During this period, Pecos and others say, they receive extensive training, including lessons on how to survive by draining the blood of rats for a quick energy drink. Older vampires also pass along their knowledge instructions for living discreetly. However, fledglings need older vampires for much more critical reasons. New vampires cannot hunt on their own and lack the skills to avoid detection, making

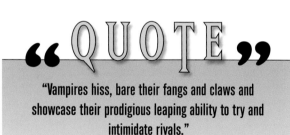

"Vampires hiss, bare their fangs and claws and showcase their prodigious leaping ability to try and intimidate rivals."

Vampire researcher Hugo Pecos explaining how older vampires dominate others.

Vampire's Disease

Bloodshot eyes, pallid skin, fangs, and other characteristics associated with vampires may be symptoms of a rare blood disorder called porphyria. In less enlightened times, those suffering from the disease were mistaken for vampires and hunted and killed. Porphyria, sometimes called "vampire's disease," disrupts the production of a substance called heme, a molecule that carries oxygen to the blood and gives it its red color. Those suffering from porphyria are marked by uncontrollable tissue, bone, and skin damage, that gives their skin a pale color and makes it painful to be exposed to

them vulnerable when not guided by their masters.

Despite their weaknesses, according to legend, even young vampires possess abilities far beyond those of regular people. For example, they are said to have telepathy, the ability to mentally communicate with one another without speaking, and telekine-

sunlight. The tissue damage can also affect the mouth, causing gums to recede, making the teeth appear larger, like fangs. Porphyria causes extreme anemia, which in medieval times was alleviated by drinking the blood of animals—or, some say, human beings. Acute sufferers of the disease may experience paranoia and hallucinations, behavior that might prompt observers to believe that the victim has become a vampire. This genetic disease, which may be spread through inbreeding, was said to be common in Transylvania and other rural regions about a thousand years ago at a time when many vampire legends took root.

sis, or the power to move objects without touching them. Within months of becoming a vampire, they gain even more skills. At 6 months a vampire can ostensibly control the weather, and after 2 years it can control animals. These skills help a vampire to feed, allowing him, for example, to cause a snowstorm to drive

Vampires have telepathy, the ability to mentally communicate with one another without speaking.

hunters to his castle. At 3 years, a vampire can incapacitate its prey through hypnosis, and after 5 years the creature's stealth and cloaking skills are so highly developed that it is virtually invisible when it needs to be. When 10 years has passed in a young vampire's life, it can rapidly climb walls, like a cockroach. By a vampire's fiftieth anniversary, it can shape-shift and fly.

A vampire over 200 years old is said to be ten times stronger than a human, and by this age, the blood drinker has probably accumulated considerable wealth. Older vampires have other advantages as well. Since they possess more skills, the strongest, referred to as alpha vampires by Pecos, are able to lead packs of younger vampires who do most of the hunting. When the fledglings catch a victim, the alpha vampire drinks first. This gives him superior strength, and lets him dominate fledglings. According to Pecos:

> Like virtually all mammals, [alpha] vampires assert their dominance through display behavior and fighting. Vampires hiss, bare their fangs and claws and showcase their prodigious leaping ability to try and intimidate rivals. Physical size and power are important but by no means the only determinant of alpha status. In fact, intellectual capacity is more important than physical prowess in determining success and longevity as a vampire.[30]

Despite the belief that vampires live forever, destruction is a constant threat to alphas and younger vampires. During fights and hunts, vampires can lose eyes and break bones. Older vampires are often heavily scarred from such activities and may be missing ears

J. Gordon Melton (pictured) has often been criticized for studying religion and subjects like vampirism, as many see as this a potential conflict of interest in his reporting.

or even noses. As these injuries take their toll, vampires may lose their ability to hunt, causing them to die from malnourishment.

Vampire Women

Although most vampires are male, according to Pecos, about 15 percent are female. However, as American religious scholar

Some people believe that there are vampires living today who are old enough to have seen ancient civilizations thrive and the pyramids of Egypt built.

Vampires

J. Gordon Melton writes in *The Vampire Book:* "The dominant image of the male vampire, frequently preying on weak females, has tended to obscure the role of the female vampires in the creation of the vampire myth and the important female vampire figures who have helped shape contemporary understanding of vampirism."[31]

Female vampires are mentioned in centuries-old folktales from every continent. Hundreds of eyewitness reports of female vampires have been recorded in Europe. In these accounts, the female vampires are described as sharing the same physical traits as their male counterparts, and they exhibit equally strange behavior. For example, villagers in Devonshire, England, in the nineteenth century talked about a farmer named Jack who was visibly wasting away as his wife dazzled visitors with her radiant beauty. Villagers noticed that Jack's wife had long, sharp, blood-red fingernails and extremely pale skin. When guests came to dinner, she was never seen eating food. One night Jack saw his wife gliding noiselessly, like a snake, toward him as he lay in bed. When she bent over his neck to give him a vampire's kiss, he tried to grab her but she changed into an eel and escaped. Like thousands of other vampires, Jack's unnamed wife doubtlessly found other victims as the decades passed. She may still be walking the world today, for there is no way to know how long a newly undead creature will stalk its prey. If such beings are real, there may be vampires walking the world today who were citizens of ancient Greece, or even witnessed the construction of the Great Pyramid in Egypt. With a heart that beats once a day, and superhuman strength, they only need the blood of living victims to remain undead another day.

"The dominant image of the male vampire, frequently preying on weak females, has tended to obscure the role of the female vampires."

—Author J. Gordon Melton discussing vampire women.

CHAPTER 3

Stopping Vampire Attacks

For as long as there have been legends of vampires, there have been stories of vampire slayers. In most societies, vampire hunters were simply townsfolk who banded together to stalk and kill creatures that were threatening their community. However, in eastern Europe the task of slaying vampires was often turned over to professional vampire hunters, who possessed animal-like cunning and, above all, the desire to commit extreme violence on creatures said to have superior intelligence, supernatural powers, and superhuman strength. In Romany tradition, the individuals best-suited for this job were *dhampires*, the half sons of vampires. These vampire-men often had physical deformities such as snub noses, no fingernails, or deep marks on the back that looked like tails.

Dhampires are common in Gypsy folklore since male vampires are seen as irresistible to women and said to produce many off-spring. Consequently, in past centuries a number of men in eastern Europe were said to be the spawn of vampires, born with heightened senses that allowed them to see bloodsuckers even when they were invisible or disguised as animals. Although the Romany feared the dhampires, they often hired them to rid their villages of vampires. These vampire hunters operated on the shadowy fringes of society, earning a living by exploiting public anxiety about the undead.

A Stench in the Air

The appearance of a dhampire in a community usually meant that a vampire was near—or at least that is what the vampire hunter told the frightened inhabitants. The vampire hunter noted the telltale stench, which suggested the presence of a vampire somewhere in the area. To find the source of the stench, the vampire hunter removed his shirt and held the long sleeve up to his eye like a telescope. Spotting the vampire, he would then command the bloodsucker to leave the village. If this failed, the slayer would attempt to kill the creature in vicious hand-to-hand combat or by shooting it with a sacred silver bullet blessed by a priest. After the battle was over, the stench would increase for a time and a puddle of blood might be left on the ground.

The dhampire's task was made easier if the vampire could be traced to a corpse in the cemetery. In such cases, the body was exhumed and either burned or a hawthorn stake pounded through its heart or stomach. Melton describes the logic behind staking: "In these cases it was assumed that the stake would hold the body in the ground. At times the body would be turned face

downward and then staked. If the stake did not work, the corpse would only dig itself deeper into the earth."[32] The meaning of this ancient tradition was modified by writers in the nineteenth century, however, when it was said that a stake driven into the heart would stop the blood of life flowing through the vampire's veins. In keeping with the belief that vampires are immortal, if the stake was removed, the vampire would come back to life.

One of the more unusual tricks employed by dhampires involved bottling the undead. This method, practiced in Bulgaria, involved professionals who pursued vampires with a bottle holding a few spoonfuls of animal blood. Brandishing a picture of a saint, whose holiness terrified the bloodsucker, the dhampire chased the creature up a tree or onto the roof of the house. Once entrapped in a high place, the dhampire produced the bottle holding the bloody snack. With no other means of eating, the vampire crawled into its prison which the hunter fastened tightly with a cork. The bottle was thrown into the coals of a blazing fire and the vampire was destroyed.

Whatever method the hunter used to destroy a vampire, he could name his price for the work, and it was often very high. Traditionally dhampires were paid with gold, cattle, or jewelry, as well as a meal and a new suit of clothes. However, the vampire hunting trade drew a fair share of charlatans who preyed on the fears and superstitions of the public.

The swindlers often worked in teams. One man would secretly visit a village after a funeral and perform vampire-like stunts. The throat of a farm animal might be slit and left in a public place, houses would be broken into and ransacked, and women were attacked in the dark. Once the news spread among terrified villagers that a vampire was on the loose, the second member of the team would arrive claiming to be a dhampire. The con men could then stage an elaborate show with pyrotechnics and staged screams, culminating in the victorious battle with an invisible bloodsucker.

Tools of the Vampire Hunter

The Romany were among many cultures that propagated vampire-hunting legends. In Bulgaria slayers were referred to either as *vampirar* or *glot*—literally, hawthorn. Since tradition held that the best vampire slayers were born on Saturday, they were also called Sabbatarians, those born on the Sabbath. It was said that they could only subsist on the meat of sheep that had been killed by a wolf, which would give them extraordinary courage beyond that found in the bravest men.

In Serbia, it was said that vampires could only be slain by professional vampire hunters who had powers that were almost magical. These slayers could play music that would enthrall vampires, creatures known to love music. The songs would cause the bloodsucker to let down its guard after which it could be easily shot or stabbed through the heart with a wooden stake.

Other slaying techniques involved playing on vampire weaknesses. For example, one skill vampires do not possess is the ability to swim—they sink like a stone in water. In addition, vampires are very attached to their clothing, such as hats and capes, which are said to give them special powers of invisibility. Therefore, a vampire hunter might try to steal a vampire's cape and throw it in a river or lake causing the bloodsucker to drown when he tries to recover it. Vampires are also very attached to their burial shrouds and garments, called cerements. A cunning hunter might wait until a vampire has left its grave and steal these items,

In this still from the movie Salem's Lot *a man attempts to kill a vampire by driving a stake through its heart.*

using them to lure the creature to a dangerous place, such as the edge of a high cliff. When the vampire climbed up to retrieve its cerements, it could be pushed off into the abyss, dying as it hit the ground.

Another means of killing a vampire involves cutting off its head with a shovel. But not just any shovel will work, as Guiley explains: "Hardware store shovels simply won't do. A grave digger's shovel possesses a certain supernatural potency from its association with the dead. A sexton's shovel possesses the holy power of God."[33] Killing a vampire this way is dangerous because anyone sprayed with vampire blood might go insane or die. So slayers who used this method were careful to cover the corpse with a cloth before swinging the spade.

The severed head must be likewise treated carefully. While avoiding the blood, the slayer must fill the mouth with coins or stones, so the vampire cannot bite anyone. The body is then disposed of in a variety of methods. It may be buried with the head placed under one arm, the buttocks, or feet. Or, the head and torso might be buried in separate locations, far from one another.

A final vampire disposal method is based on the ancient beliefs concerning crossroads, or the places were two rural roads intersect. Thousands of years ago, the Germanic Teutons built altars at crossroads where human sacrifices were conducted. Since criminals and the insane were usually chosen as sacrificial victims, crossroads came to be associated with executions. After Christianity was adopted in Europe, authorities continued to bury outlaws, including suspected vampires, at crossroads. The symbolic burial location alerted the local populace that the corpse belonged to an evildoer. But even if the vampire rose from the dead, the intersecting roads would throw its demonic brain into

"A grave digger's shovel possesses a certain supernatural potency from its association with the dead."

—Parapsychologist Rosemary Ellen Guiley on the best shovels for killing vampires.

confusion. Unable to decide which road to follow back to its village where it would seek revenge upon the living, the vampire would remain far from town bewildered by the roads leading in different directions.

Dead or Alive?

Professional hunters have devised many methods for destroying vampires as they stalk the living. However, stories of vampire encounters suggest that the best way to prevent attacks is to take measures that stop vampires before they clamber out of the grave. In the seventeenth and eighteenth centuries, this was done by hunters who opened graves and mutilated thousands of corpses during periodic bouts of vampire hysteria. These slayers looked for specific signs of vampire activity in a corpse. For example, Summers writes that the body of the vampire is normally "exceedingly gaunt and lean," but "after he has satiated his lust for warm human blood his body becomes horribly puffed and bloated, as though he were some great leech gorged and replete to bursting."[34] Therefore, a swollen body in the coffin was sure to receive a stake through the heart or a spontaneous cremation in a public bonfire. Movement of the corpse was also said to be sign that the body was either trying to escape or had left the grave and later returned. Another gruesome characteristic attributed to vampires is described by Guiley: "When staked, vampire corpses make noises in protests—even shrieks."[35]

Today, there are scientific explanations for supposed symptoms of vampirism. For example, a corpse produces methane gas that causes bloating after death. This natural gas may even cause shrieks or groans when a stake is driven into a body and the gas is forced out by the pressure. A restless carcass might also be a sign that the individual was buried while still alive. This was quite common in ancient times when sick people who were unconscious or in comas were thought to be dead. If they awoke underground they would struggle to escape their horrible fate, making claw marks on the coffin, tearing cerements, and chewing shrouds, signs of suspected vampirism. Whatever the case, scientific reasoning was not a factor when a slayer went about the business of saving a town from a vampire problem.

Warding Off Vampire Attacks

Stories of hunters tracking down and destroying vampires have provided small comfort to people through the ages. Therefore, in many cultures people devised their own protective measures in hopes of preventing attacks by vampires. European peasants in particular developed many rites and customs to keep the dead from arising as the undead. Some preventative measures were performed on every deceased person, others only on criminals who might come back to harass the living.

Many preventive rituals are performed immediately after death. For example, when a person dies in Romania, coins placed on the eyelids are said to "pay" the soul to leave for the afterlife. Once this payment is accepted, the soul cannot return to earth. Another ritual involves sewing or tying the mouth shut after death to prevent the soul from leaving the body. This forces the soul to stay in the grave with the cadaver.

A person's house can also be protected from visits by vampires. This may be done by stopping the clocks at the time of death. According to a European superstition as old as mechanical clocks themselves, stopping a clock is said to put the corpse in a sort of suspended animation, protecting its physical and spiritual

The Germanic Teutons, pictured, built altars at crossroads where human sacrifices were conducted. Since criminals and the insane were usually chosen as sacrificial victims, crossroads became associated with executions. After Christianity was adopted in Europe, authorities continued to bury outlaws, including suspected vampires, at crossroads. The

burial location alerted the locals to what type of person was being buried. If the vampire rose from the dead, the intersection would confuse it. Unable to decide which road to follow back to its village, the vampire would remain far from town bewildered by the roads leading in different directions.

integrity until it can be buried while preventing demonic forces from entering the body. Another superstition states that mirrors should be covered in the presence of the body because the reflective glass is believed to reveal the soul or spiritual double. However if a corpse is seen in the mirror by the living, the soul can have no rest and is at risk of becoming a vampire. A glowing candle placed near the body is said to provide the soul with the light necessary to find its way into the afterworld. Without this guidance, the soul might become lost, wander away, and become a vampire. The doors to the house can also be painted with a tar cross because the black sticky substance is said to prevent evil from crossing the threshold into the home. The cross itself is also a powerful symbol said to repel vampire attacks by representing the righteousness of Christianity.

While rituals concerning crosses, candles, and mirrors are universal throughout much of Europe, others are regional in nature. For example, in the Romanian village of Vrancea, attendees at funerals laugh and sing rather than cry. This is meant to trick evil spirits into thinking that a birth is being celebrated, rather than a death mourned. An even more peculiar ritual in this town involves a dance; two of the strongest men at the funeral will lift the corpse from the coffin and dance with it so that the spirits will not think the person is dead.

In Italy and Greece, crying at a funeral is not only recommended, it is required. In those countries, it is said that if a person is not properly mourned by weeping relatives, he or she will come back to haunt them, possibly in the form of a vampire. For those with small families or few friends, professional mourners are hired to weep and wail at the funeral procession, ostensibly making the deceased feel loved and wanted.

Whatever funeral rites are used, it is commonly believed that the corpse must be watched over continually until it is buried, as New Orleans author and vampire expert Kalila Katherina Smith explains:

> In Louisiana, many families still practice a custom called "sitting up with the dead." When a family member died, someone within the family, or perhaps a close family friend, would stay with the body until it is placed into one of our above ground tombs or is buried. The body is never left unattended. There are many reasons given for this practice today, most commonly, respect for the dead. This tradition however, actually dates back to Vampire Folklore in eastern Europe. In doing this, you were watching for signs of paranormal activity. If a cat was ever seen to jump over, walk across, or stand on top of the coffin; if a dog was seen to bark or growl at the coffin; or if a horse shied from it, these were signs of impending vampirism and at that point you would take steps to prevent the corpse from returning from the dead.[36]

The Cadaver in the Coffin

While many preventative measures are carried out before burial, others are meant to keep the corpse in the coffin once it is underground. For example, a cadaver might be placed face down in the coffin so it cannot crawl back to earth after it is buried. This would also help if the corpse needed to be exhumed since the gaze of the vampire is considered fatal and a face-down cadaver could not stare

Stopping the clocks
at the time of death
is said to put the
corpse in a sort
of suspended
animation, protecting
its physical and
spiritual integrity.

into the eyes of the living. However, this type of burial might false-ly convince people that the body is that of a vampire since gravity causes the blood to settle in the face. This would give the corpse what Summers calls "full and rich . . . red lips."[37]

Other methods of dealing with the dead include weighting the body down with rocks inside the coffin or tying the arms and legs together to prevent escape. Wrapping the cadaver in a knotted net was said to confine the vampire to its grave for centuries be-cause, according to German legend, the bloodsucker is only able to untie one knot per year. Sharp objects such as thorns, nails, daggers, and spikes could also be placed above the midsection to prevent the remains from rising. In Romania, a sharp sickle was often placed across the neck so if the vampire attempted to float to the surface, it would be decapitated. A sickle might also be shoved into the heart, as this is said to be the seat of the soul.

Distracting the dead is also a popular technique for vampire prevention. Filling a coffin with poppy, mustard, or carrot seeds will keep a vampire in the grave because eastern Europeans be-lieve it must eat each one—at the rate of one a year—before exit-ing. Likewise, stuffing coffins with food, such as meat or potatoes purportedly keeps vampires full and prevents them from desiring warm blood. In the 1903 book *Macedonian Folklore,* sociologist George Frederick Abbot describes using millet grain to keep vampires in the grave in Alistrati, Greece:

> [If] someone was suspected of having turned into a Vampire . . . [the] tomb was covered . . . and mil-let was scattered over it, that, if the vampire came out again, he might waste his time in picking up the grains of millet and be thus overtaken by day.

For the usual period of their wanderings is from about two hours before midnight till the crowing of the morning cock.[38]

Further preventative measures are often taken to keep vampires underground. In Romania, the ground above the coffin might be outfitted with several sharp stakes. If a vampire were to try to rise from the coffin, the stakes would perforate the vampire's heart.

Finally, one year after a suspected vampire dies, relatives in Romania might walk around the grave smoking pipes, cigarettes, or cigars as this is supposed be an effective means of confinement. If all else fails, before the one-year anniversary, the body may be disinterred, the heart extracted and burned, and the ashes scattered over the grave.

To Burn the Body

Fire has long been associated with destroying vampires. Flames are seen as a symbol of divinity exemplified by God appearing to Moses in the form of a burning bush to send him to Egypt to free his people. In Europe, fire was also used to kill heretics and burn those accused of witchcraft. So, it was seen as a powerful tool for stopping vampires. As Summers writes:

> To burn the body of the Vampire is generally acknowledged to be by far the supremely efficacious

A Hungarian Hunter

In 1746, Dom Augustin Calmet published an influential book about the vampires of eastern Europe, describing how one person, known simply as the Hungarian, dealt with a vampire problem in Liebava, Hungary:

> [A] certain Hungarian . . . mounted the clock-tower of the church, and watched for the moment when the vampire came out of his grave, leaving behind him in the tomb his shroud and cerements [burial linens], before he made his way to the village to plague and terrify the inhabitants. When the Hungarian from his coin of vantage had seen the vampire depart on his prowl, he promptly

descended from the tower [and] possessed himself of the shroud and linen, carrying them off with him back to the belfry. The Vampire in due course returned and not finding his sere-clothes cried out mightily against the thief, who from the top of the belfry was making signs to him that he should climb and recover his winding-sheet. . . . The Vampire, accordingly, began to [clamber] up the steep stairs which led to the summit of the tower, but the Hungarian suddenly gave him such a blow that he fell from top to bottom. Thereupon they were able to strike off his head with the sharp edge of a sexton's spade, and that made an end of the whole business.

Quoted in Montague Summers, *The Vampire*. New York: Dorset Press, 1991, p. 172.

method of ridding a district of this demoniacal pest, and it is the common practice all over the world. The bodies of all those whom he may have infected with the vampirish poison by sucking their blood are also for security sake cremated. . . . Any animals which may come forth from the fire—worms, beetles, birds of horrible and deformed shape—must be driven back into the flames for it may be the Vampire embodied in one of these, seeking to escape so that he can renew his foul parasitism of death. The ashes of the pyre should be scattered to the winds, or cast into a river swiftly flowing to the sea.[39]

The Power of Garlic

Garlic has also been an extremely popular method for either destroying or warding off vampires. Used for medicinal purposes, garlic was long believed to have magical powers that offered protection against the plague and other diseases. This led to the belief that vampires have an intense aversion to garlic, and people began to wear chains of garlic flowers around their necks to repel vampires. Upon burial, the mouths of suspected vampires were stuffed full of garlic. In China and Malaysia, the foreheads of children may be smeared with garlic oil in order to protect them from vampire attacks. In the Caribbean, believers cover their entire bodies with garlic to repel demonic bloodsuckers.

While some now regard the vampire-repelling powers of garlic as ancient superstition, Romanian officials sanctioned the distribution of garlic during church services as recently as the 1970s. Those who refused to eat the strong herb were regarded as possible vampires.

Garlic is also important on certain Romanian religious holidays, particularly St. George's Eve, celebrated in late April or early May. This feast day, when flocks of sheep are driven out to pasture from their winter paddocks, has supernatural associations. On St. George's Eve, like on the eve of All Saints' Day, or Halloween, witches are said to gather at midnight to perform evil rituals and cast spells against innocents. St. George's Eve is also a time when spirits of the dead are restless and might be seen wandering the countryside. Therefore, on this holiday, villagers eat garlic, rub their bodies with it, and hang heads of the herb around their windows and doors. In addition, cattle are given garlic rubdowns, and it is mixed into their food.

Vampire-Killing Kit

While hanging garlic in the window might calm the fears of some, those who want extra insurance against bloodsucker attacks can purchase professional vampire-killing kits. One kit was sold the day before Halloween 2003 by Sotheby's auction house for $12,000. Manufactured in Liège, Belgium, by Professor Ernst Blomberg and renowned gun maker Nicolas Plombeur, the kit originally contained a wooden box that held a pistol, silver bullets, and a large bottle of holy water. Two small bottles were also included, one filled with garlic juice used to coat the silver bullets, the other containing Professor Blomberg's special anti-vampire serum. A small bottle of sulfur powder, or flour of brimstone, was incorporated on the belief that the odor drives off vampires. Other items include a crucifix made of wood and copper, various blessed holy medals, a small bottle of smelling salts to revive those who faint during vampire killing, and a copy of the 1819 book *History of Phantoms and Demons* by Gabrielle de Paban.

Did You Know?

Vampires are very attached to their clothing, such as hats and capes, which are said to give them special powers of invisibility.

According to the Sotheby's Web site, such kits were probably first sold in the early twentieth century to capitalize on interest in vampires sparked by the 1897 publication of Bram Stoker's *Dracula*. These might have been purchased as souvenirs by fans of the book or by those who genuinely feared vampire attacks. Whatever the case, the label on the kit says: "This box contains the items considered necessary for persons who travel into certain little known countries of Eastern Europe where the populace are plagued with a particular manifestation of evil known as Vampires."[40]

After the kit appeared on the Internet, an anonymous seller soon offered an updated version for modern hunters. The Twenty-First Century Vampire Killing Kit comes in a black metal case with two locks to keep out unwanted visitors. There are also several crucifixes, a Bible, and a flashlight so hunters don't have to stumble about in the dark. Descriptions of other vampire kit contents are published on the Pagan Prattle Web site:

> There are 4 lead filled brass temperature released capsules. One way of destroying a vampire is to burn it in its coffin and by placing one of these capsules in the edge of the enclosure the lead will release at 255 degrees and seal the coffin shut. . . . There are [2] 18 inch copper plated silver tipped solid rods used for staking the vampire into the coffin. . . . There are also [2] 6 inch copper plated silver tipped solid rods that are also used for staking the vampire to the coffin through the hands or feet. . . . This next very important item is used in the final process of killing the vampire and one of the only known ways of keeping the undead

dead . . . a 12-inch fixed blade knife used for decapitation. . . . Last item to be mentioned would be the keys that lock this case up, they also have a cross pendant on them to keep them out of the hands of any vampire that may want to destroy the items inside.[41]

The Twenty-First Century Vampire Killing Kit was offered for sale on a popular Internet auction site. The seller tried to attract bidders by including a supersoaker water gun to spray great quantities of holy water from a distance.

Pictured is a vampire-killing kit from the early 1800s. It contains silver bullets, a pistol, a cross, and various herbs that were believed to ward off the undead. A similar kit was sold the day before Halloween 2003 by Sotheby's auction house for $12,000.

The ad for the Twenty-First Century Vampire Killing Kit was quickly removed from the auction site for reasons unknown. However, the fact that it was offered shows that interest in vampires remains strong. And as long as people worry about vampire attacks, there will be vampire hunters, both legitimate and illicit, who will try to earn money destroying the hearts of the bloodsucking demons.

CHAPTER 4

Vampire People

Vampires are traditionally defined as supernatural reanimated corpses that have broken the bonds of death to walk the world of the living, drinking warm blood from human prey. However, many vampire tales circulating today can be traced to the actions of real people who have been judged by history to be deranged killers. Authors, filmmakers, and cultish vampire lovers have melded the actual bloody deeds of these serial killers with ancient beliefs about vampires. In doing so they have blurred the line between historical fact and vampire fantasy.

As with much vampire lore, the roots of this melding can be traced to Romania, where more than 40 percent of the people believe that certain historical figures were really vampires. This is explained by Douglas Myles, who writes in *Prince Dracula,* "Few regions of Europe are as steeped in occult lore and mystery as the Slavic countries of Eastern Europe. . . . The Romanian peasantry, in particular, have clung to such beliefs since [ancient times]."[42]

Over the centuries, traditional eastern European vampire lore began to incorporate tales of the all-too-real Prince Vlad Dracula III, "the Impaler." Dracula was a tyrant who was accused of vampirism by his enemies even while still alive, and his demonic deeds have inspired countless vampire tales since his death. Commenting on the link between the real Dracula and his fictitious counterpart, Myles writes, "the two are inextricably interlocked, perhaps for all time. If the real prince had not possessed such a bloodthirsty and vicious character, Stoker would not have selected him as the logical figure on whom to base his vampire [Count Dracula]."[43]

While most Romanians accused of vampirism were average people—criminals, sinners, practitioners of the black arts—Vlad the Impaler was an aristocrat, a highborn king of the small principality of Wallachia. He was also, according to historical accounts written by Germans and Russians, the king of the vampires. His name means Son of the Dragon, which also translates to Son of the Devil. And the Wallachian prince took inhuman glee in torturing and slaying foreigners, people from neighboring regions, and even citizens of his own kingdom.

One of Dracula's legendary crimes against humanity took place on April 2, 1459, when he looted the Church of St. Bartholomew in the town of Brasov. After stealing the vestments and chalices, he burned the entire city. Hundreds of people were impaled on stakes pounded into the ground in a huge semicircle. The stakes, driven through the victims' entire bodies, caused them to die slow, painful deaths. During this atrocity, Dracula sat at his

Dracula is a fictional character invented by Bram Stoker. However, the author based his Count Dracula on a real person, Vlad Dracula III, "the Impaler," (pictured) who ruled Walachia, a principality bordering Transylvania, on three separate occasions between 1448 and 1476.

royal table placed in the center of this human misery, drinking and dining with his henchmen. The event was illustrated on a German woodcut in 1499, used to make hundreds of paper copies. This early form of newspaper undoubtedly established Dracula's reputation as a vampire. Sondra London, known as the "Queen of Serial Killer Journalism," describes the picture in *True Vampires*:

> Vlad is seated at a wooden table set for dinner, smiling ever so slightly, his hollow eyes feasting on a scene of horror. . . . [Before him we see a] writhing mass of impaled men and women, their eyes bulging, their mouths gaping open. Most have been run through from front to back, some through their spines. In front of Dracula there is a man in tunic and hat, dismembering a body. Dracula is gesturing toward this spectacle, as if giving instruction. Heads and arms lie all around, causing speculation as to what kind of meat he is dining on. Above the scene is inscribed in German: "Here begins the very cruel and frightening story about a wild bloodthirsty man, voivode [governor] Dracula. How he impaled people, roasted them and boiled them in a kettle, and how he skinned them and hacked them into pieces. . . . And many other horrible things are written in this tract and also in which land he had ruled."[44]

Following the Brasov incident, Dracula cut a bloody swath through the region. During the summer of 1460, he impaled

"QUOTE"

every single citizen in the town of Fagaras. A month later, on August 24, Vlad the Impaler outdid himself, setting what was then a record for human slaughter. After raiding the town of Amlas, Dracula's army impaled 20,000 to 30,000 men, women, and children in one hellish night. This gruesome event, coupled with other raids in the area, completely decimated parts of Transylvania, and some areas were not resettled and repopulated for more than a century. Dracula's killing does not stop there, however. In 1462, in a war with the Turks in Bulgaria, the Impaler's military raided a Turkish army camp, captured 23,000 soldiers and marched them to Dracula's castle in Wallachia, where all were impaled on a single day as Dracula watched with pleasure.

Despite his victories, Dracula was captured and imprisoned in 1462. During his six-year reign, as many as 100,000 people were impaled, burned, boiled, nailed, decapitated, hanged, skinned, or buried alive. And, "if he did not practice cannibalism . . . he compelled others to eat human flesh,"[45] according to historians Radu Florescu and Raymond T. McNally in *The Complete Dracula*.

Bathing with Báthory

After several years in prison and a decade quietly married to a member of the royal family, Dracula was briefly returned to the throne around 1475. He was aided in this quest by the governor of Transylvania, Prince Stephen Báthory, a member of a powerful noble family whose relatives ruled various parts of eastern Europe for more than three centuries. But Dracula was dead within a year. He was killed by the Turks, who decapitated him and preserved his head in honey in Istanbul where the sultan showed it to visitors to prove the horrific Impaler was dead. However, the name Báthory, like that of Dracula, would live on in the annals of vampirism.

Prince Báthory's great niece, Erzsébet (Elizabeth) Báthory, was born in Hungary in 1560 and became a countess at the age of 15 when she married Count Ferenc Nasdsady. According to London, she was as "brilliant as she was beautiful. At a time when her cousin, the Crown Prince of Transylvania was an illiterate lout Erzsébet Báthory could read and write in four languages and required a higher level of stimulation than your average blueblood."[46]

Perhaps boredom aggravated her uncontrollable bouts of violent rage, which she first experienced even as a child. Whatever the case, Báthory's cruelty to servants was boundless. While every castle in Europe had a torture chamber used to torment political and military enemies, Báthory's choice of victims was unusual. She took perverse pleasure in causing anguish in innocent young servant girls who made minor mistakes or who accidentally violated household rules. These unfortunate young women were tortured with pins stuck under their fingernails, branded with red-hot irons, or burned with molten wax.

When Báthory was 44, her husband was stabbed to death, but the Countess did not mourn for long. Instead she became obsessed with finding another husband before her beauty faded forever. After trying thick makeup to cover her wrinkles, Báthory became convinced that magic would prevent her from aging.

Before long her castle in Csejte, in present-day Slovakia, was filled with the kingdom's most charismatic sorcerers, witches, demonologists, alchemists, and other practitioners of the supernatural arts. Foremost among them was an older woman, Dorothea Szentes, also called Dorka the Witch, who instructed the countess in the ways of black magic. Dorka was joined by her mate, another old witch named Darvulia.

One day, a young maid was brushing Báthory's hair when she accidentally pulled it. The countess turned and slapped the maid across the face, drawing blood. The countess rubbed it on her hands, which seemed to take on a younger, more supple appearance. Báthory ordered Johannes Ujvary, the dwarf who was her chief torturer, to drain the young girl's blood into a huge vat. The countess bathed in the warm blood and declared it a perfect beauty tonic.

For the next five years, Dorka, Darvulia, Ujvary, and Báthory's manservant Thorko, combed the countryside searching for beautiful virgins to take back to the castle. The girls were hung by their heels over the countess's tub and, when it was time for a warm bath, their throats were slit.

Báthory's perverse quest for immortal beauty continued for five years but her skin continued to age and wrinkle. On the advice of her witches, the countess decided that peasant blood was not powerful enough for her vampiric pursuits. It became clear that only the blood of beautiful young princesses and nobles could fight the cruel rigors of time. To lure these privileged few to Castle Csejte, the blood-soaked countess opened a charm school. Two dozen young maidens enrolled in the first class. When they disappeared, however, Hungarian king Matthias II ordered Báthory's own cousin, Count Thurzo, to arrest

Dracula's reigns were brutal and bloody—his favorite method of disposing of enemies was to have them impaled on long wooden stakes where they slowly bled to death. Dracula was accused of cannibalism and blood drinking in widely circulated books and pamphlets even before his death in 1476. By the 1500s Dracula was widely spoken of as a vampire in league with the devil, and his reign was associated with vampirism, especially by those who suffered his wrath.

her. Although there had been persistent rumors concerning the countess's killing of peasants, killing royalty proved to be her downfall. As London writes, "She could have gone on bathing in the blood of peasants unmolested, because the disappearance of the disenfranchised was as much of a non-event in those days as it is in our own. But no, her sadistic machinations escalated further and further out of control until the madness had to end."[47]

During Báthory's arrest, troops raided the castle, finding a dead body in the main room, living victims pierced with holes for bleeding, and several young women imprisoned in the dungeon. The trial began in January 1611, but the countess refused to attend or enter a plea. Nevertheless, a record of the slaughter, found in the countess's living quarters, was read in court and it contained the names of 650 victims. The witches and others who aided Báthory in her serial killing confessed. Like thousand before them, they died by impalement.

Báthory was never convicted of a crime, but the Hungarian emperor remanded her to lifelong imprisonment in her own castle. Stonemasons walled up the windows and the doors to the torture chamber with the countess still inside. There she spent the remaining days of her life, fed through a small opening in the wall. After the countess's death in 1614, King Matthias sealed the records of her trial and forbade anyone to speak her name so that scandal would not be brought upon the royal House of Báthory. And while it was never proved that Báthory actually drank the blood of her victims, Myles writes, "Elizabeth Báthory is remembered in history and legend as the notorious 'Blood Countess' . . . murderess of more than 600 virgins [and] a genuine female vampire."[48]

The Vampire Butcher of Hanover

Few people can match the deeds of Báthory or Vlad the Impaler. However, on rare occasions, criminals perform deeds that are so despicable that they come to be known as vampires in media accounts and stories passed by word of mouth. These murderers may not really be vampires but people come to associate them with vampires because of their deeds. They are, Guiley writes, "far more fearsome than their fictional counterparts. They are the dread and terror of the night, the fear of death, and the helplessness in the face of the unknown. They are the evil of hell and the dark side of the universe."[49]

Fritz Haarman, born in Germany in 1879 was one such person. Haarman was an escapee from a mental institution who lived a violent life of crime on the streets of Hanover. In 1918 he found work as a butcher but spent his nights hanging around the train station where he would approach weary young travelers and demand to see their tickets. If they had none, he would lure them to his home with a promise of a hot meal and a warm place to spend the night. These young men were never seen again.

Haarman soon teamed up with Hans Grans, another deranged killer. Together they killed several young men and during the murders Haarman bit the throats of the victims and drank their blood. Haarman's vampire-like behavior continued for five years until police found the remains of one of his victims in the Leine River. A search of his home revealed the partial remains of 20 more victims. Most of the bodies, however, had been mixed with meat in the butcher shop, turned into sausage, and sold to the public. During the sensational trial that followed Haarman was labeled the "Vampire Butcher of Hanover" in the press. He was sent to the guillotine for his crimes and beheaded in 1925.

Vampire Ethics

Michelle Belanger is a Sanguinarian and PSI vampire who writes extensively about vampirism and vampire ethics. Her Web page "The Black Veil" contains 13 principles, excerpted below, for modern vampires to follow:

DISCRETION

Respect yourself and present yourself so that others also respect you. Take care in revealing yourself. . . . *Share your nature only with those with the wisdom to understand and accept it, and learn to recognize these people.*

DIVERSITY

Among us, there are many different practices and many points of view. No single one of us has all the answers to who and what we are. . . . *Find the path that is right for you and uphold this freedom for others.*

CONTROL

Do not allow your darkness to consume you. You are more than just your hunger, and you can exercise conscious control. Do not be reckless. . . . *Be true to your nature, but never use it as an excuse to endanger those around you. . . .*

BEHAVIOR

Know that there are repercussions to every action. *. . . Respect the rights of others and treat them as you would be treated.*

DONORS

Feeding should occur between consenting adults. Allow donors to make an informed decision before they give of themselves to you. . . . *Respect the life that you feed upon and do not abuse those who provide for you.*

Michelle Belanger, "The Black Veil," 2006. www.michellebelanger.com.

Cults of the Count

Haarman is but one of many vampire people found in the annals of history. In 1994, French mortician Nicolas Claux was labeled the "Vampire of Paris" after admitting to drinking the blood from the dead bodies of five people he shot. In 1998, San Francisco serial killer Joshua Rudiger swore to authorities that he was a 2,000-year-old vampire with special psychic powers. He said his strength and immortality was provided by sucking blood from his victims. Rudiger, Claux, and others like them have all pointed to Stoker's *Dracula* as inspiration for their deeds.

Since Stoker wrote *Dracula,* the story has spawned more than serial murders. In recent decades, a mini-industry has sprung up with countless books, plays, films, TV shows, and comics dedicated to vampires. However, it wasn't until nearly a century after the publication of *Dracula* that people began living as if they were genuine vampires. These voluntary vampires are not murderers, just people so fascinated with vampire lore that they seek out ways to live in the manner of the tragic, yet romantic, Count Dracula. This phenomenon can be traced to what might be called the vampirification of Western culture through the Vampire Chronicles series by Anne Rice. Guiley describes the lure of the vampire subculture: "Anne Rice's vampires are 'made' through an exchange of blood; they live immortal lives in their own bodies, frozen in time at the moment of their 'making'; they are incredibly beautiful. No ugly demons or ghoulish revenants, but creatures so exquisite and perfect they could pass for angels."[50]

Fueled by the growth of Internet chat rooms and Web sites, the number of self-proclaimed vampires has grown rapidly since the 1990s. These modern vampires point to a variety of influences, from ancient Romany vampires to Vlad Dracula, Báthory, and Rice's fictional character Lestat. These vampire lovers, most of them between the ages of 15 and 30, live the vampire lifestyle, painting their faces chalk-white, their eyelids black, and their lips blood-red. They dress in black velvet, leather, and Victorian-era clothes and wear fake fangs while attending vampire-themed parties. Rather than calling themselves vampires, they prefer to be known as vampyres (with a y), Dark Angels, or the kindred, to distinguish their subculture from stereotypical movie vampires. Whatever they are called, these people have blended fiction, fantasy, and folklore into a thriving subculture. Most members of this culture do not commit violence or practice black magic, or, according to Ramsland, drink blood.

> Contrary to media presentations, the majority of people who participate in some way in vampire culture do *not* drink blood, and many even find the notion unappealing, if not altogether unsafe. Some went so far as to call it psycho.[51]

The Sanguinarians

While most fans of the undead shy away from bodily fluids, there are a few who drink blood like the vampires of old. They call themselves Sanguinarians, a term based on the Latin word for bloodthirsty. According to the Nocturnus Web site, which is dedicated to modern vampires,

> [Sanguinarians are] mortals who have a need to feed on the blood of others to maintain a state of good health. Sanguinarians do not produce a sufficient amount of "life" energy, and therefore need

"The majority of people who participate in some way in vampire culture do *not* drink blood, and many even find the notion unappealing, if not altogether unsafe."

—Journalist of the supernatural Katherine Ramsland discussing fashion vampires.

Sanguinarians do not kill people to drink their blood but instead rely on volunteer donors to feed, consenting adults called blood-sharing partners.

to replace this energy by drinking blood, which is a high source of energy. . . . Sanguinarians have a NEED to feed. Without regular feeding, they will become very sick, and experience stomach cramps, headaches, muscle cramps, irritability, nausea and lethargy. . . . Many Sanguinarians also have digestive problems when it comes to eating regular food.[52]

Sanguinarians claim to be born as vampires. They say they first notice their unusual condition, called awakening, when they are in their late teens. When they learn to satisfy their need for blood, their bodies are said to undergo the type of transformation associated with traditional vampires. Their minds become telepathic, their bodies grow stronger, and their reflexes faster. They also develop a painful sensitivity to sunlight, which can cause blisters and burns. Therefore, they sleep during the day and feed and socialize at night.

Sanguinarians do not kill people to drink their blood but instead rely on volunteer donors to feed, consenting adults called blood-sharing partners. Often the donor is a close friend. Even so, most Sanguinarians carefully screen their donors to insure safe feeding. Blood tests are conducted at medical clinics and every effort is made to ensure that diseases will not be transmitted through the exchange of bodily fluids. Whatever the case, donors do not themselves become vampires after being bitten by a Sanguinarian.

When they are in need of blood, Sanguinarians experience a condition called the Hunger, the Thirst, or the Need. This intense feeling cannot be satisfied by food or drink, only by human blood. According to the Sanguinarius Web site: "Psychologically, a vampire in the throes of the Hunger feels agitated and empowered at the same time. Pulse, heart rate, blood pressure, and sometimes even body temperature, increase in anticipation of the act of feeding."[53]

Sanguinarians do not believe that their habits make them immortal but some say they are ageless; that is, that they do not age. They will die someday like other people. However, like traditional vampires, Sanguinarians claim they can achieve a state called torpor, an extremely deep sleep that allegedly extends their life for decades or even hundreds of years.

Although some Sanguinarians live openly, many more refuse to admit their identity to normal humans, called mundanes. They feel that longstanding hatred of vampires has produced an extreme prejudice toward blood drinkers, and they fear self-proclaimed vampire hunters might threaten, stalk, or harm them. These hunters, according to the Sanguinarius site, are "seriously unbalanced individuals who really are on some sort of holy hate crusade and intend to follow through with violence or action."[54]

Psychic Vampires

Sanguinarians believe blood is a necessary life force that allows them to survive. However, there are some who are labeled vampires who do not need to drink blood at all. According to Summers, "There is a vampire who can . . . support his life and re-energize his frame by drawing on the vitality of others. He may be called a spiritual vampire, or as he has been dubbed, a "psychic sponge."[55] In more recent years, this type of vampire has come to be known as a psychological or PSI vampire.

The term PSI is used to define the life force, sometimes called psychic energy. PSI vampires feed upon this power, which is said

PSI vampires drain the energy of unwilling victims through psychic attacks.

to be found in energy fields that surround people as well as in blood. Unlike Sanguinarians, PSI, or psychological vampires drain the energy of unwilling victims through psychic attacks. In a 1896 article in the magazine *Borderland*, German physician and psychical researcher Franz Hartmann described his experiences with psychic sponges or psychological vampires:

> [They] vampirize every sensitive person with whom they come in contact, and they instinctively seek out such persons and invite them to stay in their houses. I know of an old lady, a vampire, who thus ruined the health of a lot of robust servant girls, whom she took into her service and made them sleep in her room. They were all in good health when they entered, but soon they began to sicken, they became emaciated and consumptive [affected by a wasting disease] and had to leave the service.[56]

Such attacks may also leave the victim feeling extremely depressed, mentally unbalanced, and even suicidal. After experiencing such attacks, it is said that the victims themselves may become psychic sponges sucking up the life force energy of others.

Because of the ancient fears of psychic vampires, doctors in past centuries warned against letting small children sleep in the rooms of aged individuals. It was believed that the old people could prolong their lives by draining the energy from the young ones. This is based on the belief put forth by nineteenth century medical researcher Laurence Oliphant who wrote in *Scientific*

Religion, "Many persons are so constituted that they have . . . the extraordinary faculty for sucking the life-principle from others, who are constitutionally incapable of retaining their vitality."[57]

Like Sanguinarians, psychic vampires believe they are born with their particular traits, often discovering their vampirism during their teens. Michelle Belanger, an author and self-described PSI vampire states that "if someone is a true psychic vampire, taking energy is not a choice. It's part of who and what they are."[58] They believe they are afflicted with this condition because their souls originated in a reality or dimension different from the one familiar to most humans. According to Belanger: "Souls that have come from a reality outside of this one may not be compatible with the natural energies of this place [earth]. They may also operate at a much higher frequency than is typical to this place, thus accounting for higher energetic 'metabolisms.'"[59] This creates a hunger within the psychic vampire to obtain life energy by draining it from others.

To obtain PSI energy, vampires exhibit a number of familiar behaviors taken to the extreme. Ramsland describes one such person, Carly, and the destructive methods she employed to feed on the energy of her unwilling husband:

> While he tries to do his job he must also keep track of his erratic wife, who constantly changes her hair color to look like various movie stars, throws childish fits, makes up fantastic stories, manipulates men with her body, and thrives off of attention. She recklessly puts her husband's career at risk, and then makes a deal that forces him into a mental hospital under such heavy sedation

"Sanguinarians do not produce a sufficient amount of 'life' energy, and therefore need to replace this energy by drinking blood, which is a high source of energy."

—The Web site Nocturnus, describing real-life modern vampires.

that he becomes a zombie while his career falls to pieces around him. When she finally helps him to get back on his feet (only because she needs him), she's ready to start her manic phases again. . . . [Carly is] spirited, free, eroticized, electric, energetic and beautiful. She drains [her husband] again and again and nearly destroys him. . . . Most of us know someone like this and we've experienced this vampire's charms, as well as the inevitable destruction that follows from their needs, lies, manipulation, and demanding moods. They tease, provoke, and exploit high drama to create an impact. No one is safe with such people.[60]

According to Belanger there are several types of psychic vampires. The first is known as a Darwinian vampire, someone who values her own survival above all, stealing energy without permission. If she did not soak up the energy of others, she would get very sick and experience stomach cramps, headaches, muscle cramps, irritability, nausea, and lethargy. The Darwinian method of consuming energy is considered unethical by PSI vampires, who define themselves as "sustainable vampires," those who only feed off willing and capable donors. Belanger, who puts herself in this category, defines this type of energy vampire:

Sustainable Vampires make the "noble sacrifice" of enduring hunger and privation in order to protect others from their needs. Practitioners of Sustainable Vampirism will feed only upon consenting donors even though these are rare and hard to come by. When donors are not available, Sustainable Vampires will limit themselves to ambient feeding, a technique which draws in the loose, free-floating energy given off by crowds. This energy is plentiful but not very sustaining and, over a long period of time, it fails to support anything more than minimal functionality.[61]

When sustainable PSI vampires reach the state of extreme hunger, they will go into survival mode and become Darwinian if they must. They involuntarily become energy vacuums, or black holes that suck the life force from whomever they meet. Therefore, ethical PSI vampires try to maintain a balance between their needs and the needs of donors.

While PSI vampires and mass murderers like Vlad the Impaler have been part of human culture for thousands of years, vampirism has entered a new era in the twenty-first century. Although some researchers maintain that there are about 500 supernatural, immortal vampires walking the earth, tens of thousands participate in what is now widely seen as a New Age lifestyle, joining up with Sanguinarians and psychic vampires on the Internet. With this surging popularity it appears that the allure of vampires, like Count Dracula himself, will remain forever immortal.

NOTES

Introduction: The Bloodsuckers

1. Quoted in Gabriel Ronay, "Vampire Slayer Impales Milosevic to Stop Return," *Sunday Herald* (London), March 9, 2007. www.sundayherald.com.

2. Bram Stoker, *Dracula.* Mattituck, NY: Amereon House, 1981, p. 16.

Chapter 1: An Ancient Creature

3. Montague Summers, *The Vampire.* New York: Dorset, 1991, p. vii.

4. Quoted in J. Gordon Melton, *The Vampire Book.* Detroit: Visible Ink, 1994, p. 5.

5. Summers, *The Vampire*, p. 17.

6. R. Campbell Thompson, *The Devils and Evil Spirits of Babylonia.* London: Luzac, 1903, p. 286.

7. Quoted in Melton, *The Vampire Book*, p. 321.

8. Richard Burton, *Vikram and the Vampire: or, Tales of Hindu Devilry.* New York: Dover, 1969, p. 243.

9. Bob Curran, *Vampires.* Franklin Lakes, NJ: New Page, 2005, p. 157.

10. Emily Gerard, *The Land Beyond the Forest*, vol. 2. London: Blackwood & Sons, 1888, p. 185.

11. Quoted in Summers, *The Vampire*, p. 27.

12. Quoted in Summers, *The Vampire*, p. 173.

13. Quoted in Summers, *The Vampire*, p. 173.

14. Quoted in Summers, *The Vampire*, pp. 27–28.

15. Quoted in Melton, *The Vampire Book*, p. 76.

16. Curran, *Vampires*, pp. 157–58.

Chapter 2: The Living, the Dead, and the Undead

17. J. Scoffern, *Stray Leaves of Science.* London: Tinsley Brothers, 1870, p. 350.

18. Quoted in Summers, *The Vampire*, p. 183.

19. Quoted in Summers, *The Vampire*, p. 183.

20. Summers, *The Vampire*, p. 142.

21. Rosemary Ellen Guiley, *The Complete Vampire Companion.* New York:

Macmillan, p. 6.

22. Guiley, *The Complete Vampire Companion,* p. 6.

23. Quoted in Guiley, *The Complete Vampire Companion,* p. 6

24. Quoted in Guiley, *The Complete Vampire Companion,* p. 7

25. Quoted in Guiley, *The Complete Vampire Companion,* p. 7.

26. Quoted in Manuela Dunn Mascetti, *Vampire.* New York: Viking, 1992, p. 65.

27. Katherine Ramsland, *The Science of Vampires.* New York: Berkley Boulevard Books, 2002, pp. xi–xii.

28. Ramsland, *The Science of Vampires,* p. 25.

29. Hugo Pecos, "Vampire Sociology," Federal Vampire & Zombie Agency, September 19, 2007. www.fvza.org.

30. Pecos, "Vampire Sociology."

31. Melton, *The Vampire Book,* p. 691.

Chapter 3: Stopping Vampire Attacks

32. Melton, *The Vampire Book,* p. 165.

33. Guiley, *The Complete Vampire Companion,* pp. 37–38.

34. Summers, *The Vampire,* p. 179.

35. Guiley, *The Complete Vampire Companion,* p. 29.

36. Kalila Katherina Smith, "History of Vampires in New Orleans," New Orleans Ghosts, 2007. www.neworleansghosts. com.

37. Summers, *The Vampire,* p. 179.

38. George Frederick Abbot, *Macedonian Folklore.* Cambridge: University Press, 1903, pp. 218–19.

39. Summers, *The Vampire,* p. 206.

40. Quoted in "Vampire Killing Kit Sells for $12,000," *USA Today,* October 31, 2003. www.usatoday.com.

41. Quoted in Red Wolf, "Bargain of the Day: 21st Century Vampire Killing Kit," *Pagan Prattle,* July 28, 2005. www. prattle.net.

Chapter 4: Vampire People

42. Douglas Myles, *Prince Dracula.* New York: McGraw-Hill, 1988, p. 13.

43. Myles, *Prince Dracula,* p. 21.

44. Sondra London, *True Vampires:* Los Angeles: Feral House, 2004. p. 301.

45. Radu Florescu and Raymond T. McNally, *The Complete Dracula.* Acton, MA: Copley, 1992, p. 261.

46. London, *True Vampires,* p. 303.

47. London, *True Vampires,* p. 304.

48. Myles, *Prince Dracula,* p. 221.

49. Quoted in London, *True Vampires,* p. 37.

50. Guiley, *The Complete Vampire Companion,* p. 178.

51. Katherine Ramsland, *Piercing the Darkness.* New York: HarperPrism, 1998, p. 13.

52. "Sanguinarians," Nocturnus, 2007. www. nocturnusonline.net.

53. Sanguinarius, 2007. www.sanguinarius. org.

54. Sanguinarius.
55. Summers, *The Vampire,* pp. 133–134.
56. Quoted in Summers, The *The Vampire,* pp. 134–35.
57. Quoted in Summers, *The Vampire,* p. 134.
58. Michelle Belanger, *Sanguinarius,* 2007. www.sanguinarius.org.
59. Belanger, *Sanguinarius.*
60. Ramsland, *Piercing the Darkness,* pp. 191–92.
61. Belanger, *Sanguinarius.*

Books

W. B. Bartlett, *Legends of Blood: The Vampire in History and Myth.* Westport, CT: Praeger, 2006. This book covers the long history of vampires including their origins in ancient times, the eighteenth-century vampire epidemic, and modern beliefs, with a focus on witches, wizards, and other undead creatures of the night.

Bob Curran, *Vampires.* Franklin Lakes, NJ: New Page, 2005. Explores the rich diversity of vampire beliefs from India, Sweden, Ireland, Romania, Albania, Malaysia, and elsewhere. Discusses ancient legends, modern lore, and a variety of interesting details about bloodsucking monsters from dozens of cultures.

Alan Durant, ed., *Vampire Stories.* Boston: Kingfisher, 2004. A collection of excerpted vampire stories, including classics such as Bram Stoker's *Dracula,* Arthur Conan Doyle's "The Adventure of the Sussex Vampire," Anthony Masters's "Drink my Blood," and Jane Yolen's "Revelations in Black."

Peter Haining, ed., *The Dracula Scrapbook.* New York: Borders, 1992. A unique assemblage of material, including articles, newspaper clippings, photographs, and memorabilia about Count Dracula, vampires, and vampire films, books, and shows.

———, *The Vampire Hunters' Casebook.* New York: Barnes and Noble, 1997. Details from the case files of real-life vampire hunters who encountered men who cast no shadow, night stalkers, beautiful bloodsuckers, and vampires disguised as investigators.

Bruce McClelland, *Slayers and Their Vampires: A Cultural History of Killing the Dead.* Ann Arbor: University of Michigan Press, 2006. A thousand years of vampire hunting, trapping, and killing with stories from the Balkans to *Buffy the Vampire Slayer.*

Erin Slonaker, *The Vampire Hunter's Handbook.* New York: Press Stern Sloan, 2001. A field guide for modern vampire hunters, with an emphasis on humor rather than horror. Full of information needed to become a skilled hunter of bloodsuckers including types of creatures hunters might encounter and helpful hints on where and when to find the undead. Includes a list of phrases to help hunters communicate with vampires and an official Vampire Hunter ID badge.

Bram Stoker, *The Illustrated Dracula.* New York: Viking Studio, 2006. The famous story of Count Dracula illustrated in color and black-and-white by two leading comic-book artists.

Web Sites

Paul Barber, "Staking Claims: The Vampires of Folklore and Fiction," 2007. www.csicop.org. A well-researched article about the reality of Vlad Dracula and how myths and legends commonly associated with him have distorted the historical record.

Robert Todd Carroll, "Vampire," *The Skeptic's Dictionary,* June 27, 2007. http://skepdic.com. A site maintained by a re-nowned skeptic who questions the validity of vampire beliefs and provides links to related subjects such as spiritual vampires and transubstantiation.

"Count Dracula Legend," Romania Tourism, 2006. www.romaniatourism.com. A Web site sponsored by the government of Romania with details about the life of Vlad "the Impaler" Dracula along with photographs of his castle, forts, and related sites.

The Coven Organization, 2007. www.thecovenorganization.com. Billing itself as an "online vampire research and news portal," this site features articles, blogs, historic information, videos, poetry, humor, and stories about present-day vampyre culture.

Elizabeth Miller, "Dracula's Homepage," 2006. www.ucs.mun.ca. A site hosted by an author and internationally recognized expert on the novel *Dracula,* with many articles about Stoker's life and characters, vampires, Vlad the Impaler, and the Transylvanian Society of Dracula.

Hugo Pecos, Federal Vampire & Zombie Agency (FVZA), September 19, 2007. www.fvza.org. This site claims to represent a secret federal agency responsible for controlling the nation's vampire and zombie populations while overseeing scientific research into the undead. It contains a great deal of information about vampire viruses, biology, sociology, and myths.

Sanguinarius, 2007. www.sanguinarius. org. A worldwide communication, information, and support network for all blood-drinkers, PSI vampires, and those who practice the Vampyre lifestyle, set up to "defend individuals, organizations, and publications within the greater vampiric community against discrimination, and threats to their personal safety and welfare, peace of mind, freedom of expression, freedom to practice, right to free association, right to exist peacefully, and right to equal protection and treatment."

Bram Stoker, "Dracula," Literature.org, May 25, 2005. www.literature.org. An ebook of Stoker's classic book about the bloodsucking count from Transylvania with links for each chapter.

"Welcome to Dracula's Castle," Dracula's Castle, 2007. www.draculascastle.com. A Web site dedicated to Bran Castle where Vlad the Impaler spent his days torturing and killing thousands of people. Many photos of the interior and exterior of the castle, constructed in 1212, along with information about Vlad and general information about Romanian culture and history.

INDEX

ABOUT THE AUTHOR

Stuart A. Kallen is a prolific author who has written more than 250 nonfiction books for children and young adults over the past 20 years. His books have covered countless aspects of human history, culture, and science from the building of the pyramids to the music of the twenty-first century. Some of his recent titles include *History of World Music, Romantic Art,* and *Women of the Civil Rights Movement.* Kallen is also an accomplished singer-songwriter and guitarist in San Diego, California.